Earliest Worlds

Earliest Worlds

TWO BOOKS

BLUE GUIDE

and

OF SUN, OF HISTORY, OF SEEING

Eleni Sikelianos

COFFEE HOUSE PRESS

⌐ • ⌐

COFFEE HOUSE PRESS is an independent nonprofit literary publisher supported in part by a grant provided by the Minnesota State Arts Board, through an appropriation by the Minnesota State Legislature, and in part by a grant from the National Endowment for the Arts. Significant support for this project came from the Jerome Foundation. Support has also been provided by Athwin Foundation; the Bush Foundation; Elmer L. & Eleanor J. Andersen Foundation; Honeywell Foundation; James R. Thorpe Foundation; Lila Wallace-Reader's Digest Fund; McKnight Foundation; Patrick and Aimee Butler Family Foundation; Pentair, Inc.; The St. Paul Companies Foundation, Inc.; the law firm of Schwegman, Lundberg, Woessner & Kluth, P.A.; Star Tribune Foundation; the Target Foundation; West Group; and many individual donors. To you and our many readers across the country, we send our thanks for your continuing support.

COFFEE HOUSE PRESS books are available to the trade through our primary distributor, Consortium Book Sales & Distribution, 1045 Westgate Drive, Saint Paul, MN 55114. For personal orders, catalogs, or other information, write to: Coffee House Press, 27 North Fourth Street, Suite 400, Minneapolis, MN 55401.

Good books are brewing at coffeehousepress.org.

⌐ • ⌐

LIBRARY OF CONGRESS CIP INFORMATION
Sikelianos, Eleni, 1965–
  [Blue Guide]
  Earliest Worlds : two books / by Eleni Sikelianos
    p. cm.
  Contents: Blue Guide — Of sun, of history, of
    seeing.
  ISBN 1-56689-114-9 (alk. paper)
      I. Sikelianos, Eleni. Of sun, of history, of
        seeing. II. Title.
  PS3569.I4128 GB58 2001
  811´.54—DC21   00-065891

10 9 8 7 6 5 4 3 2 1 FIRST EDITION
PRINTED IN CANADA

ACKNOWLEDGMENTS

BLUE GUIDE

Some of the poems in this series have been published in *Grand Street, An Anthology of New (American) Poets, Sulfur, Talus, Poetry New York, The Colorado Review, Trafika, The Hat, Downtown Brooklyn, Swerve, Mentor* (in Slovenian), and in a collaborative show and accompanying book with the sculptor Peter Cole, both called *A Book of Ease / A Small Book of Unease*. In addition, a small selection of this work was published under the title *from Blue Guide*, in the PNY Pamphlet Series. Many thanks to the editors and curators of those.

Thanks are due also to the National Endowment for the Arts, which provided time, to Paul Hoover and others via Intersection for the Arts and the James D. Phelan Award, and to the friends who have read these poems and offered help and support, including Tim Atkins, Brenda Coultas, Laird Hunt (my nostrum), Lisa Jarnot, Heather Ramsdell, Leonard Schwartz, Cole Swensen, Anne Waldman, and Elizabeth Willis (for reading them aloud), and thank you, Lorna, Dan, and Serena. To Barbara Guest, and her genius.

OF SUN, OF HISTORY, OF SEEING

Many thanks are due to the editors of the following magazines, web sites, and anthologies, where some of these poems first appeared: *Arshile, Bombay Gin, Fence, Blood & Tears: Poems for Matthew Sheperd, New American Writing, Boxkite, XCP: Cross Cultural Poetics, Skanky Possum, Venice, alyricmailer, Duration, American Letters & Commentary, NYCPoetry.com, Verse,* and *Talisman* (thank you, Garrett).

I owe these poems to a number of people; among them, MM Lautréamont and Proust, who buried me in their mistranslations. And to the many who have fed these, wittingly or no. Please forgive my transgressions if a poem (or its title) belonged to you.

Thank you to Marjorie, and to the Maison des écrivains for the time to work. To Alice Notley, for asking why, and for making me understand poetry more deeply.

⌐ • ⌐

⌐ • ⌐

— . —

In all the Disquisitions you have heard concerning
the Happiness of Life, has it ever been recom-
mended to you to read Poetry?

To one who has a Taste, the Poets serve to
fill up Time which would otherwise pass in
Idleness, Languor, or Vice. You will never be
alone, with a Poet in your Poket.

—JOHN ADAMS, TO HIS SON

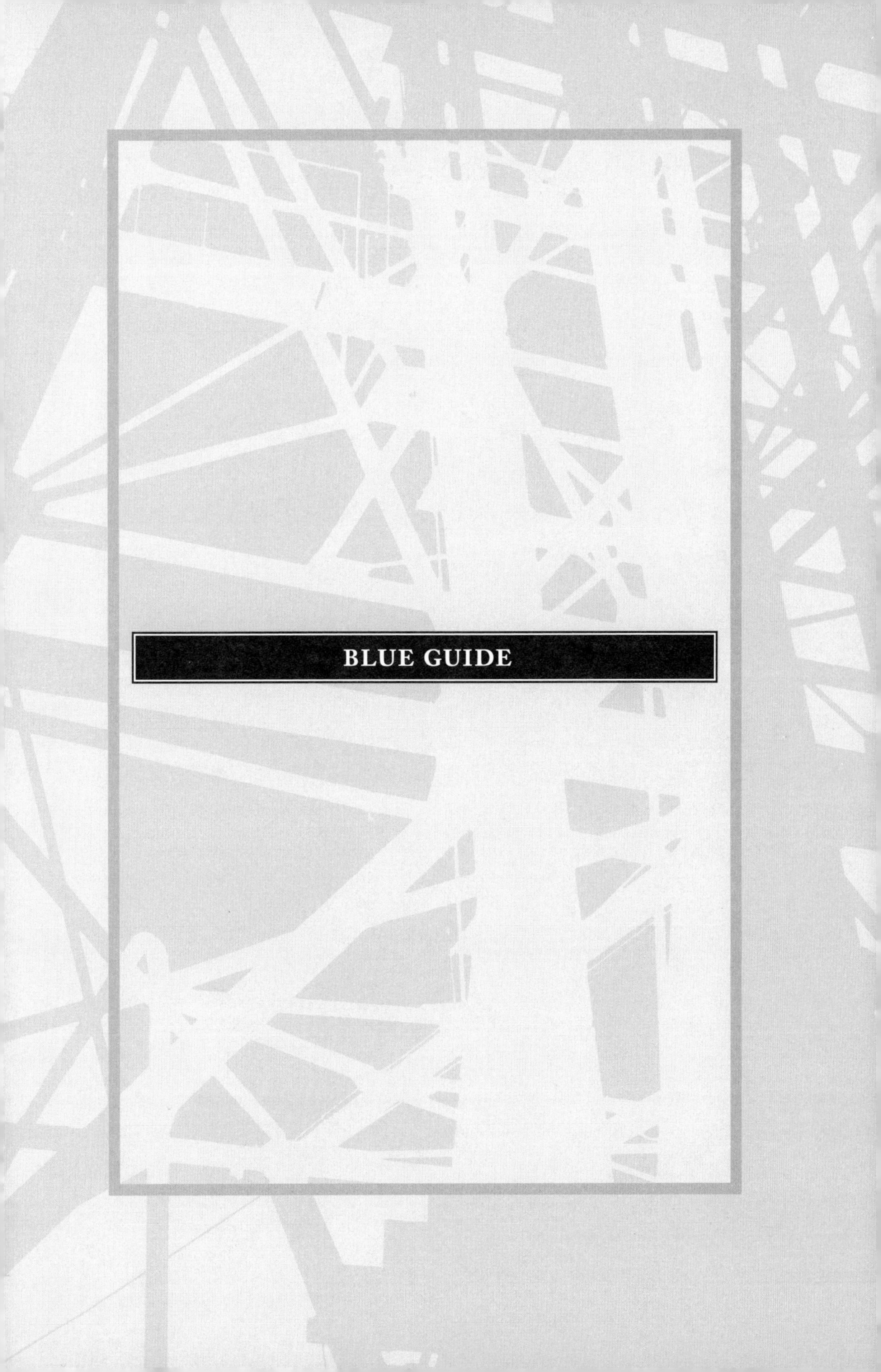

BLUE GUIDE

CONTENTS

Let the eye

which sees all

the simulacra

of the sun on

the water waves be a

b, *the*

diameter of which is defined by the eyes

placed at the antipodes over the circle that divides

day from night on the surface

of the earth

—LEONARDO DA VINCI

IT IS NOT ENOUGH THAT THE BUDS have come out. It is not enough that it goes a few degrees warmer in the world. The waiter in the park is trying to read my mind. Or is it the garden, is it the water or is it, is it. The little steps through the gravel. Then it is spring, and the tourists have begun to fill up the city like a box of nervous arms and legs. Shout at the top of your compass (sun), dream your dream on that hilltop town I have dreamt before, sometimes I ride my bike. First I go up, then I go down, sometimes I go up or down again. Sometimes there is a town, sometimes a small walled city, sometimes a drugstore and a stoplight to the left. All of it melting or frozen: a milky sun, weak as a dime. Sometimes a small window looks out at an angle on colors (like dandelions carrying their yellows), sometimes I go walking, walking to get there. Then it is spring, and the tourists have begun to fill up the city like a box of chocolates (melting), and as soon as it all melts, men and women are thrown from their seats; and cars shatter. All the voices the city winds up, a crank-up, an off-key box. Where are several thousand seconds? Waiting to collide.

Matter has been Blown
off the Surface
of this V   i   s   i   b   le Star

In my collection of gluons whose color adds up
to white:

a time the universe

was the size of a darkening
string; a quark,

an antiquark, red + antired, green + antigreen, or blue =
white. A glue ball, really— (Are there any

infinities left?) Yes, yes, they still unload the crates
of Coca-Cola in the winter
morning sunlight, some third graders' milk cartons in blue

plastic bags waiting on the street
corner. What are they waiting for? (The trash
collectors.) I will have to eliminate them—the yellow
styrofoam lunch boxes stacked together, oily, glistening—Listen:

The earth together
with all its inhabitants, all demolished and not-demolished things, is
out there

hissing.

The Stone I was Bothering

We found one of the world's stones outside.
I discovered it with my open eye.

In it was manifested a capacity to stop
the circulation of my blood, force-to-force.
For that small scar, who would
want one — "she would because a scar makes us

foreign to us." I had a scar on my left
cheek which I remembered the story of
until I could no longer see it and now
I forget.

Just the same, I have proof

of kissing-fires conned into the kiss & life-in-
                            peril for a quarter
hour or a quarter more, a mute
score for the
composition of that. The seat of sore:

inside my mouth or a pine cone at
the bottom of the brain. In the morning light enters
the eye, the body

there,
under the influence. Thus, spake
lights and the sky's zoo of ob-

jects and activities (meteors, clouds whipped into giraffes) while I waited
nearby, knocking
on Jordan, on J, or Jack   Who

can say the temperature in the heart

is not the same
as the hottest stars (one thousand million centigrade) Heat

responds to the motion. "If we knew how the body was made
we would never dare make a movement again" (Flaubert), but even he had to make do
with visible hands.

DEAR FLAUBERT,

How many enemies? What anemone has
this hand,

this "making the dumb material talk"? I'll arrange it into a glowing
city built from sound and turn it around. Earthly things will adore
earthly things, other things will echo. Bread is called cake here.
We'll cause crime, Goldengum, time over time. Let them offer a
prize of sixty—I don't care—They offer curtains through white air.

The Most Beautiful Theorems
of the Theory of Animals, Numbers

No john can exceed the mellow
bath of one square root

of the light the insects form
in the tints & forms of the sleeves of trees. And in the fits,
the dark, and the dark

starling turns
the whole startling

head into the mouth,
head,
night,
flesh. If
Massachusetts
Carolina Ohio could walk
& talk I would tell them : rain

is made
of places trading
with the flesh. What is flesh

through the bush

of far pines & eternal
sky? Congress

of asters, polymers, free
to start carbons, cars.
The jewel is strange, Animal, shaved

by slip-
knots, gulf-

lightning, radiation. Therefore shall I unsex my dress
rising up like an antelope, bending

down like a pear? Ocelli, ovipositor, in my dreams of affixing
the glittering twigs

back to their sticks I did conceive
of the bathing forms and sleeves of
conscious-
ness.

Everybody in the Country's got a Clubfoot

is how he heard that work
in which each thing is identical to itself, each suburb

with its microfiche, a blank on the tax

form filling a Herculean labor of numbers with no place
left for doubt tripped out, "where every neurotic
conflict is seen to be part of human
fate as a whole" and mixed with snow, embroidered

into this bit of garage-like outlandishness.

Still, I can hear cars hum in your back, a single
will on the scattered emotions—some-

thing bluish "shot with rose."   Those
are the singing bombs on the Avenues, a History

of human labors printed in softer tissues;   In the opening

threshold a Field
of dark-like fire from which

Light

"introduces itself
to strangers"

As a child, I had an eye which was applied to my head according to the accompanying scale of a face, full-grown. Who made my eye as big as a bow window, five feet long? Things would fall in. Splinters, chairs. Forgetfulness altogether came over me, bending reeds. Something went hot and hissing along every one of my wrists. First it was the handling of the spokes tight as a harp-string, then the wide world, falling.

Chapters

of I Define the Darkness Correct

— *The Speed of C*

"Human, have you heard?

'Cruelty which began with man will end with him,' " but who

was authoring rain
from the other extreme

of the dome ?   Where it rounds itself out
into a knot of blue ?   The sky is a heavy
mass which flows

between blue and absence
of blue. The atoms
which went into the snoring

towers—the buildings with wings in their cages—will the
suspended bridges continue
directing themselves over the quays ?   Between the blue

lines and the red was
the incredible Achilles tendon, the astonishment
in a woman's ankle while moving

from one

place to the next, on the in-
side, to the left, to

the right, which-

ever way the   eye
meets it   a weakness
behind the
knees, smudge

in the coal
cellar. Think
dark about galactic dark now   Think   What is least

acquired in science:
The face of a man

who no longer recognizes himself
falling

falling often

in fury resembling a creature in the briar-thicket.
All this time he thought he was only composed of a good

maximum
quantity of particles—such as the gold

chain engulfed
in the crease of his neck.   Dizzying   white thinking dark or red thinking
fingers airplanes silver streamers over the sky, the surfing

eye. I will soon be
situated

somewhere
here, very near an artery of six star-
like avenues, Sweet

Atmosphere,
the stone

would like to exempt itself from the laws of gravity.

~ *Joy's the aim*

A man was leading us through trees. We saw darkness in the
kinks in the mud, the sun

that dropped in her hair like
screeching fires   in the dream "I Define   the Darkness Correct," the day

wrinkles into the dream where the man was

leading us through trees. There, we were lost of us, boxed
between the poplars, with no room in between   Nocturnal thicknesses
          of a brilliant

childhood packed into nights
and days repeating   who never made a pact with shadows or

Evenings, dusk
fell on like a blanket of sad riding me
or my bike through the fog

Dreams of a ruined state had not yet taken body——When was I

          torn to the clear
          from tenebrous force

or the "center of earth" which hits mid-body;   erase all trace
          of before or after
  (simultaneity)   darkly confirm
                    fissures

27

It was just the atoms that held up for the moment

Who put the plug into humans
I could find none   common measure nor   take body   to chase
cars into
stars. What is this troglodytic
fur treading my wrist? (It's a wig.)

Now they are digging up the garden & we can hear it from the hole. That one was
always losing her grip. Soon, the ubiquitous apple
tree, prey to the "green membranes of space, scientific perfection of world vs. world
sucked up in a swirl of lighting, or a thin layer of tissue over the bones right
down at the inner part where the

marrow is. One unit of logic & a million
                                    take body; What happened
in your personal historical?

            The dried-out glue we used to
            sniff

            thinking about, like money
            before that she
            and after that she spat   That

            animal is resting.

            cream of gold
            cream of silver, evil

vegetables, I mention you
as soup

Backyard bard, teens
slamming into fences, girls
with holes in their
stockings, fat
ankles, say
uncle (not me) a girl's a
hole we all know that

                                                It

        sounds like a war outside or in
). Someone \ perforate   the cavity.

I will take all responsibility for my birth.
I was my own accomplice & adversary.
I must sting the light as it soon appears that being born
is an infinite proposition, a crisis I

suffered in my verbs
in the limits where a word can enter
into solid existence, a word can enter
into relationship with other words
heated to white-hot, a virgin eye thrown over
two-storey homes, Six-
teenth & Mission Streets, 10-
dollar threshold, a "crystalline
ray" brung to the human ladder & dreams fell asleep on Canon Perdido near the
handcrank washtub and under

on all my bodies ... Then, & ... nights

and days repeating a heart in forensic

relations; ... Then, & I was young: ... Suddenly.

It was just before Easter

when they took ether from us
they took ether from us
because they discovered light

was both particle & wave, fructi-
fying itself, traveling
solo, & today in the metro was the thumbprint of a shadow just above

or just below the clavicle
of a woman

traveling there. The thumb decided
to describe
the arc, like a

bee-
school, apiary

string made straight across some
grasses and the shadows of a
throat as light

as 0.07 Suns

              at the
    eye's horizon.   of
          wavering
            flame.   of the

writ and devastation, ripping
the administrative veins from electrometric trees; who makes the
glue and the gold
stick to the light, make-shift code
of shattering

TV fire.   Not the nightish
ghost in the windows, & howling.   Not the
howling, howling.   Just little
whispers of ether like a silent
tea kettle. Like the kitchen
about to explode. Like returning to the dark,
night, "I find my lovers sleeping
next to me," history writes.

Where is the center of human
suffering? A tight pit at
the pit of the city with the brighter
flesh radiating outward. Or inside
out, the dark rings around the city moving
in and in? At St. Denis? A man
by the freeway picks black-
berries, and no wood-

lot bloomed without song.
Fields of wild mustard outside the sub-
division mushroom, each

one a Flower Beneath the Foot / Sudan / cut off the hands
of my dream when waiting for such things as "Good
night" at the end of the beginning of sleep. Pledge

allegiance, he said, or the pain
starts again. I lived by my book but they asked me to move my body

through a series of movements called "work"   What is the name
that is the game, of the essences of objects of pain? I is another
name for the labels

of laughable
[detours], contents, i.e.

Night Road Work, my lyric work's distance from mere existence like a bus en route
    to an air-
port or a mul-

berry which comes

from a tree

but doesn't eat you. It itself is edible if plucked
  from the branch where it might be attached in light or in
    shade. A shadow sits
      on the ground but a dog or a person sits some-
        times in a shadow which might

          be moving. Pain

        moves through a body like shadows
        detached from the limb
        of a tree and if plucked what

        radiated outward in shade or in
        light, in pain? The phosphor is mulling

over the productive tension political or social between
resistance and pleasure, a quiddity

in five aggregates of atmospheric reading Something starts up

in the hippocampus rearranging

the windows on stars or our wives as they are, or we race
to the beginnings
of cities,   stretch
like the slow-moving lemur   Our husbands' backs
spread over the shoots and the fields of the lots and in between buildings
between   dark   between   cities

⌒ *Joy, also*

Suddenly a STONE shaped like a
heart, a real heart, as busy as rush

hour is, the heart one I found in
a box, with blood, in some-
one's book.   a STONE shaped
like a stone like a heart-
shaped habit

                              the habit
of a mind minding a hand, excuse me it was writing
a history of myself and

                    traffic lights, waitresses

                    the windows house
                    little fires on the hills at
                    sundown

                    see, see the world is incarnate (the hand) it wrote

                    a bird his head now long & growing

I remember a distant
country, a far
    far shore
everything was white &
exploding
    & the trees were
thick   with leaves

AGAIN, SEVERAL YEARS PASSED. While now upon so wide a
field thus variously composed, I embraced a distinct geologic
period prior to human me. Driven to the remotest drawers and put
me in a rocket / locker, I'm no longer this acres of living *figurative
coriolis* force. I'll now make bold to show: I don't carry such a small
gulf, before the continents broke water, I don't measure so much in
my accelerating shoes. Upon the sites of rivers and cities the bro-
ker sells me land at a million an inch. He claims it to be in the
vicinity of the lustrous bones of buttery angels. Blue card or green?
I'd be as air, I'm so rich, but now we're down in the books as owing
for the flesh in the tongue I talk you with.

Book of Tributes: Cosmorama

Look—wool

in which: gold stars we got
for trying. It's like tying the genius of July's columns from a rug of light a five-
mile width across the surface of this place, a hotel garnished
in infinite
States: easy. In Indiana, there was an early revival technique with biscuits & gravy. New
York, the river had gums under its stubble-butt teeth, and under its teeth, teeth.
    California con-
fuses building green

from pomegranate peel & madder leaves. France: rhetorical

baptisms in helicopters, spinning the phenomenal gas station
behind the château. And in France they're always drunk, and in Scotland, and in
Greece, that model of industry and good driving. In England it was eating e-numbers
over Blake's bones, marigolds, a blinking eye of grass, and an empire nailed on sheep.
Elsewhere, the "Help! I live here!" people, and the "That was when" when
I was very young, before I had come

from devouring a lunch of air. Then there was lights.

Lights

(Roubaud)

Light is the point of boiling

Things are worn out light

There is light, Texas, Nevada

The total of light is: the world, maybe

It's of light you speak? America?

Light is the first corporeal

Everything that right now envelops
a thing in shadowy thought, uncorporate
or night, like
smoke or even dust or burnt
pollen can be slowly substituted

There is light & lights

What came first, lightish or lights?
Sun or sun? O o sun.

Makes tenebres faint, shadows
pass out

FRESH FROM THE LATITUDES OF BUCK-HORN HANDLED bowie knives, the atmosphere's quarrelling again, and I have renounced ever landing. Marco Polo was never here on his chersonese crucible steed measuring poverty in Montreal. When the Earth-stop happens from the eaves of this good Golden Ear, there will be a redtide, red pipe, rip. There was an inverted visitation during which we could not tell the difference between heads and feet. Seeking to remove ourselves from that eye, dismasting. Yet if I become here and there electric and frowned upon by batteries, unplug me, a forcible narcotic, like the story: sleep.

The Typical Hand

In my left pocket is a hand.

As you can see
it is cutting & dividing the parts

of an animal body with a knife
and scissors, etc., in order to see & consider them
a-part.

Now it is rejoining with needle and thread what
had been separated (synthesis).

Now it is taking them apart (seam-ripper).

Now hand is extracting foreign bodies (exeresis).

Now it has added and applied what was wanting (prosthesis).

What?

"Hand has something to say," he said.

Hand is not limited
to looking at the face, tongue, excrement

taking the pulse, assessing the heat
and damp of the skin.
Hand will now educate the eye
to capture hidden symptoms

with finger pressures, types of pinching, deep

and superficial stroking. Hand will describe kinds of bandages,
plasters, sutures, post-operative healing

Hand will cut you now.
(This is the Hand of God.)
The muscle from bone,
muscle
from bone
to distinguish
a fake from a fraud, blood
from a stone.

Hand is helping the wounds of epic heroes.
Hand is full of dignity and informed of labor practices, fracturing
wishbones. Hand knows
about the Managing Brain & Tricking Craft, how to split / crush
ulnas, carve or quarter
a lamb. Hand is
rupturing something maybe

Maybe your spleen. Hand is severing something now maybe

your head.
Hand, o hand

is doing the work
of the hand (manual) Hand
is so sensitive, intelligent, hand
is capable, cupping you. What
about the question
of universal diaphaneity? Hand is
so keen, cutting you now.

THIS (my) brain-truck, a knot of numbered wasps: the bright bones floating at the base of the skull; orbiting veil of gray around. Come in the lowest form of love, and I will kneel; and roll on the stunning ground; and yet and 2 will walk; who is darkness leaping out; (I) applied a system of light; as of a crushable gold (glob); muffled in a sun thrown bold; of a blinding (electricity beholden); in the crux of an extending hand; take the precise bearing (of light); hearts are congenital: (their) smallest cells pricked; inverted; who, hands or hearts, magnetism-shot.

Most of my life, this happened: each evening as dark descending, a descending sense of doom. As soon as I often left the house, I begin to sweat. Riding my bike through blackbirds at dusk, it descended upon me. Toward the small path around the marsh. You know the one. Like cutting the watch band off so that every time I tried to see the time, time fell. It fell in the water along the path and no longer tick-tocked. In the metro it's very far to this stop. There's a man playing a guitar, it's electric, he is always right here in this bend he's old, I know this song but can't remember. Is it "Stairway to Heaven" or something about lemons, I wish I knew, I wish I knew him I give him money. Everyone is waiting in the hallways everyone moves back toward the train. It's hot no one talks no one takes their jacket off Someone is pissing into the metro again. My face drops, that's gravity descending. There was a woman carrying a wheel.

Thus, Speak the Chromograph

Saying: One night in a cloud chamber
I discovered a thing: that a thing (I used to have a crown
of light)   a thing could be more
than True, and more again

than False, a thing
could carry its name

with a ticket of lights
called Possible: In a cloud chamber, particles are betrayed
by movement and water vapors

leave trails. Discovered: when matter and its antithesis come
together, a disappearing
flash of light: (our share of night to
ear) (I mean what I say): In contempt

of the Law of All
Excluded Thirds: laws are not
symmetrical in the forward and the back
(of time). On which side
are they stacked? and the sky also

(is what made Hart Crane
so crazy in the heart) continued to pile up
clouds without account, a mass of gasses with nothing

scribbled under them; a song in the middle

of the crystal
cavatina. We hardly had any bones then. Did
Hart Crane have bones? If so, which kind? And

how far down? It was written
in the boned hours, the Book of Weeds, a treatise on leaving

the house at dusk, when all buildings have already had time enough
to fit themselves back into shadows. As if there were only:

dusk-to-dusk, between dusk-and-dust
where no animals asserted themselves

as separate from the day, and the night
comes again, as it always

has done. The fact was that
I could not follow the map—because the Book

of Nature was written
in math's un-
certain language, author of black

rains, why the naked
eye
unclothed
can see

between math's limits
why
a baby's bones are soft

as pudding when first let out
of the water & take

a long time
to harden, you can flatten
a newborn

's skull by placing it
on a board, the death-hole
of the cranium takes

6 months to close

and then grow brittle

In describing the last
arc of the last
circumference: I miss(ed) that halo.

(How long it took to understand rivers

run toward the sea)

POLAR CITADEL, CHARMED CIRCLE OF DECEMBER: Now that the light has changed, everything's different, whole buildings appear where they were not. Like that hole in the sky there, through which a finger of light is trying to escape. Or is it an eyebeam, handed down at an angle? I suspect they are carefully diagrammed—but that tree seems to be flying off sideways. One trouble: many days there are half a million people hiding outside the door, others another five and a half billion riding (the small system of light). Today I saw a bird—a regular dun-colored small-to-medium-sized bird hanging by its leg from a thin rope in a tree. Its wings were spread. Gertrude Stein said, "Dear Christian. You are very sweet without hope. Hope is for you." Then there were trees being finger-pressed by light, and the small bars of bronze between the leaves.

City between cycles of light

This is or is not the middle
of a big American city with the killers

lurking everywhere; we walk
over bridgeways, trestles; cars rush
across the thin air rushing 54

seconds more
of light each night and the children
smelling of metal

and smoke. They're here too. Bloods are
moving—even here the sky is up

to something   What comes
out of our mouths—is that still dust and

tobacco juice? Eerie, our humming,
insect-like & human but elegant

grievings, gracilities Other cities
are doing & bragging but we are
being, other cities

are vacant

but here we have our personalities
at the zoo, the bright
fabric stretched, confabulation

of birds and children yelping, the I-am-a-camera phenomenalistic
parody, ethnography, our laughable attempts at winking, the littlest weight there is (the eyes)

NOW THE BELLS HAVE BEGUN, and the flashing cameras. In this garden, there is a fountain that looks like a column of moving water. This is what it is; it looks like itself. In the middle of winter, on the coldest day, all the fountains of the city have frozen over, and they look like cakes with icing. "That's not something you see every day" says an old woman on the bus, pointing. But no one wants to eat it—it no longer looks like itself. What makes an ice fountain tick? Ice. Now the waiter has brought my sugar and although my pants are dirty (he is nice to me and) I am happy to watch the little sparrows rummaging about in the dust with the no-light light. "Light"—" . . . which is not an axe."

I ALWAYS TOOK SHADOW for shelter, not "umbrage" for anger. Shadow: "dark zone created by an opaque body which intercepts the rays of a luminous source (above all that of the sun)." There is shade, partial shade, to throw or cast a shadow, of houses, trees, or leaves. There is no coin of shade in this place; a hemisphere plunged in it. In my arena: a darkened cone is cast by an asteroid / star. Who was once made in the shade, a man makes some; in the "shadow of the old oak," lock him up and throw away the key in places and places of, prisons of shadow or shade. Misprision. To put in silver's shadow (safekeep). In the "shadow of" there is no more me to speak of her or you. Now I will seek, now I will give, now I will eclipse your sun. Gray, a color serving to shade. We cannot see these contours. Earth of Shadow, there is something in this picture, it carries an inconvenience, a threat, a black stain. There was a light sky which made a dark shade on the lips. Certain details were left out (in shadow or in shade). In the night doubly crossed by shadows and the deep street he remains in shade, in a situation obscured, unknown, in that which weaves in darkness, secretly made; forgetfulness, I will come out of this shadow. Relative shadow casts a body on the surface of a (another) body. Afraid: the lengthening shadow I carry up hills. Of inseparable friends: like a body and its Chinese shadow on a screen. You cannot tell the race of this person. Meridian shadow, the shortest, that at noon. A hint, a trace. The shadow being considered a changing apparition, transitory and trompe l'oeil, pain and pleasure pass (a shadow). Prey to shadows, fragile. Seeking, kissing shade. All is accorded to a presence or absence of sun. In certain beliefs, apparition of a person who walks in death. Feeble reflection (that of summer). Thin. Its mouth is smaller.

THE DEVIL WAS KNOWN FOR DOING PORTRAITS, presenting the mechanical outlines, the vacant profile. He got one of his authentic abortions from a Chinese drawing. Around the Poles are the revolutions of the bright lights that first defined him. Changing form from all the known horrors of a half-known life, to any that could be found in a Western clearing; he stood for a moment over the eaves eyeing the vast corpse he had made.

—HERMAN MELVILLE

Worn like a corsage

In this country
of agreeable skies   Second me,   Third me — in the Courtyard   of the

Dead, torture
the hummingbird between your teeth, enemy

of snow — No matter — my legs is
      a pale branch of seed &   "I   will I swear I will"   walk

sans teeth, sans eyes   with a toothbrush & a laptop, so under so over the salted alpine
Alps Rockies yelping

I could less touch (being of good / bad milk)   the ridge   of
Danger

Let me

remain still
in the ice-fair, the true blank

        of an eye
      athwart the heart
as a puny tilter

E—is
        nothing am

   Copse me in these   fits, Rose,
   at an instant   Lame me with it

       make a testament as worldlings go — to rush
an atom; I'm so full   of matter, rushing

the barrier
of psychological speculation—from goods and pleasures, Rush,
abandoned of the velvet
            friends,
                    Heave off

these small animals cluttering earth
                Hem away, boys,
        to kill them up & tie this

leaden note   unto
the sweet bird's throat

O quanta qualia suntilla sabbatta
How mighty are Saturdays

oh happy just to walk
on the tips of his toes

sorry sorry for the bike that falls   over, giving in
to gravity—Old men come down

to smoke cigars gray-haired   Mothers carrying rag dolls down to the river

When 15 and the center of the world

There is no one other here to sit by the river and smoke and giggle, no one
but loves him
in the eye anymore, the bodies

hurtling

through said small world. I forget the words he uses
to speak to himself, the radiating tongue   dumb-gilded
The eye forgets   of color   I said

come, thought
come, thought of me of him
come, little thought of her of me of
sand, my sand adding one to one &
all
there is

come, thought, to fasten done to done

and I will no longer let
the adversary kiss you at his ease

HERE IS A STORY about the world in which no air was left, the "Season-on-the-Line." Oxygen, only within a less-wide limit. I heard the knitting needles fifty miles at sea, exceeding the more firmly final visual sweep. How that sparrow cuts a sudden path in front of us, into the devious zig-zag of the world's circle. What makes a sparrow tick, a pig tock, a sun stunned? Today, the sun was being eaten in the sky, finger by finger, about halfway there to an almost perfect state of perfect interior androgyny. One singular creature, that one (sun) dunked in some hooped ocean, a lost sheep's ear loitering. As the vein is presumed to expand or contract, but never exceed its limits, so was I conjured to myself in one set time; my life-spot, with a little expanding elastic tourniquet, a string marked by some unprivate cypher (history) moves forward and back.   Under the conditions of a manufactured (made) human, I ventured out against every atmospheric influence to divest myself away from this place, St. Mark's (St. Sulpice), & I am laughing & sticking my tongue between my teeth—those stupid baboons, these skulls shimmying; where the fiddle plays play I the sedulous ape. Under duress, a ball of free will drops from the hand. A distant whimpering; something about moonlit ships, & I forget to observe the evening descending over the fountain with light playing behind the stone lion what happened next. We could smell the water. Any tendency to trip, settled bodily down into blue, a boat along like a horizontal boiler, busts. Who divided this ocean into districts? The mind deleagued from the body. The mind, with no object to color.

— . —

You can be King of the Corners, holding down the fort and looking out toward the plains. In the middle of Earth, rocks fall apart and citizens wonder: are humans made for following orders? If man is the greatest natural wonder, what? Time turns to that motionless minute "read at the back of the animal's eyes," tarry rebellions of new-formed teeth start up, for $6.00 an hour other generations, other creatures, begin in the slime. Soon, unfortunate music starts up as some errand-boy throws down sex between the seas, handles the sun into some stunned girl, and rocks and coelacanths all come charging.

The brambles of cavalry (Quamash)

the ana-
cardiacious sumac
      mango

pistachio and
      varnish trees
are missing

a center between
      the diverging
branch

of the river which loses itself
      in sand and

      and the events
which were misplaced

in time, the fruit

of the family being likened
      to a bird's heart which explodes inside the bird's
        heart like

proton explosions sixty tons under
      the waters

        of TNT . . . i.e.:

A, H, an alphabet of bombs
    invented beneath deserts & unfolded in limbs in wings
        of cities, off atolls and coral
            reefs. A to Z, a compendium

made itself known to the messengers
    of maths, the wearers of theorems in scarlet

numbers. They have hermetically sealed
    the mouths / of bearers / of wonders / the trash

cans in this city, each a badge
    of detonated dark. It's a trash

led lockdown. The cops are on the lookout. It's pirates. Blackout.
Leaning into the precipice
    of a deadly

question

mark, I forgot
    the wise-lessons, severed mathematics

sweet filter like a freshet
    from the cradle. There was something

vague in the head, an I-don't-know-what, and thick
    as smoke. Rising out of the radiation
        the repeated testing of the H: a monster

    400 feet tall with foot-
        steps 60 feet long. Let us call this creature: Godzilla. That lizard

treads beaches, squares (Pythagoras's

friends), learns to leap
   degrees that lead to trig's altar; no longer needs
      Earth's goods, carried

on the darkling wing, concise by the chain

that makes the iron shine; Luminous
      triangle (hypotenuse), run the test

of the largest prayers; by dazzled
      potencies of supreme we wrenched the treasure out

of chaos's entrails bursting
axioms & hieroglyphs signing off

the latent breath I traced
an ascendant propeller on the

burning paper. Other borders, other creatures born. He has his orders. The people

will run. On the paper, in the cave
   of St. Desire, I was saved
      from the clutch

of matter Before
      we learned to eat

the death camass
      in the deep woods off I repeat

this train
    will not leave

the station, the night
    tortoise riding an iron

horse, & spit-

shining the floor. On the paper in the dream I was trying to make another purpose-
ful propeller, a word

garment between alpha
and O. for before we wore

the warbelt inside out but
the letters   the letters would not fit. In the coal-dark
cold-dog corral trapping

neutrinos in our sleeves, scientifically speaking the we I speak of became
    a candidate for missing
       matter, rivers

of it moving; the stars are
    burning gas, the black

back-
    ground is the sky.

The Secret Life of J.K. Huysmans / parataxis

I'm only glad   I have this body

because I had another one in a blaze of saints I searched the phrase

ductile to dream   a word to carry "dream" on its back

What nightmare are we entering (what ca- price): Spit

insects   imitating arabesques Marvelous beast

Sly bandit, the compact platinum   that Nature gave

a triple-tongue;

luxury   of pain,   of detail

This lang. can hardly suffice, suffer; the opening field of   artifice

will open largely on a Gluttony for words Succulent jewel;

Barbaric; Do flowers imitate their artificials?

Rose-of-Raw-Meat Marvelous beast Super- fine / Super-

fly;   Be, glide past   a tear in what

Paradise [unacceptable paradise [unacceptable   analogy] (the avenue:

red   yellow   blue

a lexical obstacle   a lyric one   a rupture from

melody;

I will soon make my animal tears into something you can recognize, out past my habitat of synapses. When such odds and ends as us swirl up on this floating ball tied to the sun like an ancient bird caught at its ankle, bring a sugar cube for the ghosts of all that's left of earth's first firsts; divest the body of its intricate dresses, and I'll make you a path made plain by elbows aflame, I'll lay my head on your heel and feel the weight of that matter. In the afterimages of a quantum leap, let fly that crashing when the lights come on at dusk. When was the first memory of a woman and a man, of a woman and a man waiting, waiting? I got this off the mouth of our plates: What's left to eat? Roofless space, vacating time.

Chapters

— *Touching the Original Matter*

The elsewhere is the region of time-space that does not lie in the future or past light cones . . . *For example*, if the sun were to cease to shine at this very moment, it would not affect things on Earth at the present time because they would be in the elsewhere of the event when the sun went out.

—A BRIEF HISTORY OF TIME

⌒ i. Paleomagnetism (Stars) —

The contents of a body:

Where iron is: (Meteorites, magnetite, magnetism, from lithosphere to batholith):

From an ending star, iron becomes the dust that clumps to make a solid planet

(In the beginning) the particles acted as minute compasses and settled
in the direction of the Earth

Below the oceans, under the continental granite, a crust of basalt

Even allowing for bones, the density of our bodies is closer to air or water and

Light can't travel through rock. Some stones have made their way up

to the surface: Dark, heavy peridotites, formed
at high pressure in the deep field, the slowly circulating mass
of molten nickel-iron, white-hot

As bloods in the arteries move, motion
in this part is affected by Earth's rotation
lunar, solar pulls

The world's deepest hole could not touch this mantle

— *ii.*

the arches are the binding, the windows
are the books. Here, a cult
of relics or kisses. A flam-
boyant rib is for flames in the middle of
of (duration). Dear

     wish you were here
     to watch the chronologue
     of time pour in like a slide of a dog
     howling and an accordion smile. That would keep night
     inside night's accomplishment   Cold comes
     in through a window falling over the most famous

          cumulus; — "STORM, WHAT IS YOUR
          deluxe amount of cloud?"

Even now the skies
would like to cream You see how cream but
naked is when hung
by the

[Light] & gently

stroke the day

⟶ iii.

Work out the story
of a star's life by picking it up at different stages. Nobody ages
in front of its eyes.

  Stars are grown,
      loose- &
    tight-limbed lights

around us, lidded

golds. He: helium, first-born atom, seen

by the sun's light, turn
hydrogen to helium to make the blob shine: a star.

— *iv.*

Night.

We enter the fish. We eat.

Through the small bones like flakes.

It is raining.

The windows are no longer known as "blue," but "Blue
milk coming through the window." It is a huge house built

of a huge halibut. Or is it sea bass? In two halves. The larger apse is of white
flesh, the smaller, smoky black. There are beautiful curves in these backs, siderated
on the stone plaza

Eventually the increasing temperature and pressure of the dying star
force the change into heavier elements.   The collapsing heart blows the
star / the heart

apart   Light up the final tatters delirious

hope

v.

my knees,   The sun is a hooded mass arguing

through the garden, a grunting weight. Its shadow
has climbed to this place, your eyes' light

of luminary error; the brambles
of which fiery couch! We know the property of rain

is to wet, to take advantage of a black
hole bursting into the x-
world with radio light stealing, and everything
dominating starlight; wild

veins, smoke-
flowers dodging
trains, a moving bird of luminous light (light)

lodged in each

of 86 heartbeats   tells this self to shadows; Helium   hmm   who can say how
stars
run out?

⟶ vi. Ordinary gloss: Arcoplasm / Traceries

The Practicing Ruby:

    Rose window, a
    wind-eye the shutter
to keep out such varying cold, but still see, say

a waxpalm and wave-trains, the labor of ramified lines
vaulting the tabernacle, flying buttresses

as the framework of an organ bundles fibers into little beams and rows of cells that
bridge inter-

cellular space making
fingers and mosses, extending, as in mosses, so in fingers, across cartridges, over cavities

of blood or stone or air—

Here's the deal,
    The shapes we knew
    knew our hands, The acred
        joints

        of earth's knuckles
        bossing up the ground—

vii. Laboring through Winter (primer)

I am (not) not always what I knew
I am under what

what star ?

which cage of pale plastic rushes ?

to wash our lives as clean ?

I don't want to polish my shoes, not my feet

I think the world's asleep (under the kennel's edge

under Throat-of-the-Wolf, Marsh-of-Mud-Faith
under sulking fires, the thought-
executioner's gentle tire, under cruel garters, under the Night—

Star-wheels had worn the place
Stars are
impersonators senators just as a small coal-
hand can throw off a cloak, so moved can be made
of sun, sun of rain, or if not, not at all below
the croup of hills posing as themselves in indecisive pale

They did not include our cloud
not not any cloud

Yet even now, we will allow clouds to be white, white
to be green; I declare I move

from here to there from which you can de-
duce the sun. It

Shone.

Campo santo

—Non ai, voir, mere, non ai, non!

I learned to say no in the old language
studying at the Night-school

of Electricity on Rocket Street
Before I got my eye put out

on a teeth of forests—No

to the angels, no to electricity

No to pretending to read when the ear is open

the Pearl

of venery, this vertical blanking
about ten lines outside the TV's frame

No, no, for what is not No
hid by umber & alcove

SOMEONE IS SEWING NEXT TO ME in the next room and I can hear their feet working through the walls. Will they work long into the long night now.

If the leak should double on her (on me), desert her in a body. Tell her not to sing for what, in case any what should be discovered.

The decameron

Don't think in sleep I am
absent

in this repeating

NIGHTS

as in

NAMES
owe nothing

to me; Don't think

I am ready

to be skeletal AGE

glued to my neck BUT

WHAT am I here blind to (for)
I am always blind

to something i.e. Everything
we see is made up

of 90 chemical
elements tunneling

through the energy barrier

and a blue square applied to the body of the EARTH:
and if they said; here; live here; six billion of you; and
we did; ready

to smile in the morning and shed tears at night; and tomorrow and in the evening and
the next day again; at the dark

and keyless light, shapely galaxies, smoky galleons monkey around I'm standing close
to Earth's surface studying the nighttime sky without the aid of science

To the fireball that started off
the universe some
15 billion years ago: HELLO

from us with origins in dust

Of the True Human Fold

& I am of the skull & corpus vertebrata hiding inside
the microscopic structure of a bone

& my osteoclasts will tear it down & my osteoblasts will build it back

& I am of chordata & endoskeleton hiding inside
a star the buildings of dust that stuff

& I am of hominidae & anthropoidea Look my 2000 cc brain capacity

& this is my heart's atrium & the a. of my tympanic cavity
& here is my hepatic vein
& here my oral hood
my vestibular canal   organ of Corti
my homo sapiens' larynx   mons pubis
& here, my axillae armpits milk-lines along each side & I am hiding between
the dawn ape & nuclear fission

If you can't find me at the Lake of Aegyptopithecus
Look for me at Child of the Hook, my black-bone burning

my blank
spine

— . —

THEY ARE CHASING ME HOME AGAIN before I've intended to go, far before they have packed up the carnival. No ferris wheel being dissembled. I won't go. I won't go before the barkers have drained their flume and all the barbes-à-papa have been consumed, till the last line of summer eats up the trees. There is that lion devouring a man again. There are the American girls with hairy legs. They are trying to make me go home, having assembled themselves as sirens and decoys. One morning was the bluest morning I had ever seen. It was this.

"The birds are at their highest thoughts of leaving"

My eye can't fix you
in the whole white
nuance of light

or

Astonish myself to find you
such as I am; swimming;
separated from each

by a field delimiter; who rises
to look for the light-socks folded
into a satin stain-drawer;

I warn you: Nothing solid
is built on me; I can't design
prudence for the first time

Each day, from my joints

I raise toward you

the accents of a

Stop this commerce
Stars belong to you

Because you know the detours
of a heart; (Shut up or) Tell me

HERE WE ARE ON THE PLACE ST. SULPICE again looking onto the stone lions who are looking onto the water again. Light plays. I am sitting in the front café and I can't see myself in the glass except when people pass. When people pass they block the light (light plays). I wait for myself to appear. People must pass, and they do with heavy hands and shoes. Your mother says she is never herself in dreams, she only sees herself, but I believe I am never more myself. A dreamer is only an angle of herself in a sliver or a drape. There is a boy throwing a blue cylinder into the air which he catches spinning on a string tied between two sticks. Your mother says the lions don't look majestic, they just look like themselves. Your mother is sitting next to me even so I write her a postcard on the back of Ste. Chapelle with a red ceiling which she says is blue, and stars, *experience is a hoax,* all the people we speak of, a life moving through the subway elevator or a world, seeing the girl with blonde hair on the stair, another boy with his hamster, or TV animals. A dreamer is willing to reflect our most jewel-like and distorted fashions, a sudden walking of the real earth circumstance, that is, over it unto death   The peripteral rows of obsidian pillars around the whole funny jungle   This circumference would not be the animals' shadow but real: real.

The well-tempered clavicle

This is the story of

the boy who almost admits he fell
into the Seine clacking cymbals between two small fingers
about the distance I want to say
between air & air

& the small windows replaced
on the face of the water, the water
was moving toward lights

in a shoulder of tunnel, throwing
sparks off the collar, a swallower
of flames The tiny petticoat throats of the River Look
each pane swallowed frame-by-frame This was written

in The Book of When I was a child I dropped a knitting
needle into the Seine it descended its course under

bridges & corpses under The Buttresses of Our Lady
of Spiders The legs of the church are
Arachnid, of Barbary, in any old
church of Europe you can hear the voices ascend more

beautiful in repetition when the math was so exact the voices
mixed with the roof

WHEN THE THINGS WAS AFIRE behind the houses projects spires. When I was all sold for the lonely Western I heard the heart motor in the middle. It woke me up. I couldn't get it to shut up. I began arguing, nodding out. Between me & the morning—tindering sheets. And all the little birds was there, poking holes in the night, piping out songs.

The river's which river's why

Georgics

<<Unvex the messy clouds (with hearts on sleeves)
<<All creatures follow
—Kindling
<<Kind after kind

(said the dream)

Watch me
walking into the Seine
making as an adult
on its iris-edge

wood-clefted in the golden dorsal, my mother
growned big & alone. Had we not

betrayed the farmer then the cow, might we

still live on Milk Street with a bit of Mary's
shirt next door. I'm keeping to the beau's
stratagem, a foot in the best
barn builders in American song   I don't want this

house in Cheapside anymore. They're asking me something
from the accordion again   I won't
give in. If you want the car of snow

driving home through the windshield

I will bring it to you
whipped by a column of break-

neck wind, the splintering SUBJECT
of the catallactic regime

Swell yourself toward night
hands near blue & full

of lakes
of breaking

lights

— . —

As a result, some astronomers believe they may be just as much in the dark about galactic dark matter as before the concerted search began; like the

learned astronomer looked up (the skies) and fell head-
long, a grace-
ful ditch.

Under the tremoring table
(eighteen stitches)

Rail us past trouble
to stolen

ease

with force
The sand

and
flawed

evening
Under

us is

   land.

Of lithe
Earth
spins its

light

reaches
below the surface of such brains

before
the mind

received this smooth
tablet thus what

were we

pre-
    light
who remain

silent

motionless in this
vivid picture of earth's
creatures, its

sets of leaves and acid ices,
addled by shocks, moving solid

to liquid in the shadow

zone; falling

remains of planetary

bodies, stony &

metallic; the bull
that shakes this

cup; and sea-

floor spreading.   Water, open.

At river
's ledge, 3
green King-

fishers sit
on the wire where
all I thought

was dead.
Curving round
the marsh

a skunk
fox
we hit

none of them and think
all that's living here

"on earth's
soft coat." All
we thought
dead, not.

The palace of thunder

In tissue & in chalk
l'étonnante

rich encounter under the
desert corridor

& the little boys tumbling down hills
& the little light girls

who the sun
who

Inflamer

soft hammer

Light

OF SUN, OF HISTORY, OF SEEING

DEDICACE

In his étude on Late Bathers Proust discovered
a small patch

of fat swimming at the back
of the ankle, just above the heel, like a dark gold

fish, lovely gift, perch from which a small-time
sparrow

could do a lot of looking around. I think Proust invented memory
in a hive of glass that was his head. And using light

as a blockade, I led my way
to victory—an elevator

in Proust's neck.

CONTENTS

Il n'est desir plus naturel que le desir de connoissance. Nous essayons tous les moyens qui nous y peuvent mener. Quand la raison nous faut, nous y employons l'experience.

—MICHEL DE MONTAIGNE, "DE L'EXPERIENCE"

ESSAY: *13 Pressure Points Inside the Skull*

(I was) (previously) incapable of establishing a link between one phenomenon & another
like the colors & shape of the bridge in the water in front of the susceptible
　　(unknown) spectacle　Later,
numbers responded to calculations　It was distracting　Numbers obeyed

It disturbed me that THINGS is divided into sectors and this one says MONEY and that
　　one says (K)ING

between one phenomenon &
another like the colors and the other and the shape of the (bride) in the water I loved
a man I could not recognize

I would have liked to live in a less dangerous world
where things resembled things
had I, I
taking sustenance from leaves might I, I
kept mistaking myself for Napoléon
on my way to the subway with a
implant up my sleeve

I shoved all my blood & bone
into one rough foot
—the left—no, the right

Nobody, come to me I says
So, nobody comes

inside were closed letters,
atomic, reversible & shining

and then we // we then
the reports shattered

so I wrote RECOGNITION
I wrote RECOGNITION to perform in

ESSAY: *Of Space, Stainless Steel, Of Gifts*

EXCELLENT EARTH, magnet jar, now
where are you taking those sandals?

in the geologic dent, earth-rent with stones
magnetically thrown

from space; flying flowers
of Earth; my hand folding inside my hand

folding inside the earth
seems to be missing

its feet, its
prismatic car; with contact limited to:

shave the wing on
on the human

wing on

the body keyhole
can't start

start the engine; the mechanic
hum of wheels Of the wheels of life in him—

an *I-am-sorry* image / mirage / a trompe-l'oeil body / traitor
vigorous pincers braid the optic waves I would not

disturb the natural situation
of my mouth to make my teeth go away nor

with an oblique eye deroute
the mortal intelligence: Fear; pay

for my sleep with cash the atmosphere's
couch cousining air I'm neither The sun

is neighboring feeding off ether & light a starveling
in vertical flight I could not

rearrange the stretch marks on the wing

the sling (won't fit)

the slingshot split the Most
Ideal designs itself slowly over another

sky an indecipherable
fold Look sharp winter

journeys on this surface Skin your eyes Now

hold up a broad bright husk Now hail the act

of nailing gold to the mast, the rotation
of crops in twilight, the gloves of

silence that voice me Let me
touch this axis

ORIGINS: *From Hasting's Arms*

In the first days
I saw "born" and "grow" in the grass

seeds falling from the apple

the power scissors: shade
   & beam   dark-circling   cutting trees
         leaves accomplicing leaves

the boy's hands—too—light falling
when the rain made arrange around me

I found some charm for them
what sensed me for an astral (actual) body

cramping the
ceiling knotted up toward the
     A (tree) (A) house you
couldn't live in if

the sweetness of the next return or room but prior to
    to arrival then

the anger did & author of my sad & gold
who comes "out of my own hands," shaking

ESSAY: *Naked at the Root-Post (joy)*

That night, there was the pleasurable feeling
caused by the acquisition or expectation of good; gladness; delight

In the same evening that rendered it impossible (joy) could hear something
taking place (I will make it) (take
place): a joy, a jug,
a juggernaut, the cause
of joy
hurled under the wheels and
crushed. Nature

carried the naked struggle from the inside to the
      from the outside to the
(I can't remember)   but to change a heart

little by little
till it requires
what it can't

At the last minute joy was removed from me
(I will take it / back)   even if a heart changes suddenly   Nature

charged & destroyed
the phenomenon / (joy)   The heart which at the moment

misrecognizes me is resolving
to describe an occasion of declaring love to explain the diverse forms of chagrin

(but it is no longer there, the heart all

chemical and all
I started with joy later joy
was a heroic stance to be taken at breakfast or dinner

It is not at all certain (who can be sure?) that joy arrived
that no one no longer loves joy or waited for it
if it is at all joy the same joy, if ever there was.

Only, it takes time

(for what?)

My exigencies on time are not
less exorbitant than those required by a heart but

I am in a hurry to have this end

ESSAY: *On the World as Will or Will Not*

Accident, come

from the side of the walk I forgot

to look, from a center (called, the heart). Collision.

Flower the absurd error of growing

to abstract from (my) (one) self (love) / to enter it ablaze

I had a nerve that often cried "help" (a) (world) (a)

a body too "funny" to keep sickness a secret

Each evening was said to be   the threshold

of an intact me which would begin tomorrow

— if I could have written a message on a rock & thrown it through the window

There was no window,

there was no window, and there was no rock.

In a period besides existence

I tried to undo what seemed indivisible // As soon as one sound arrived

in my ear / another

replaced it // Put the head

of one on the body of another, mixing

attributes and blending names till the faces

slide from street to street   flying by the seat

of my pants whistling

into an empty .22 I found in this pocket; it's only New York.

If life no longer had for a goal // but tender //— throned at the back / of the taxi — //

who would decide //an ear is / closed / or open / The subway, a pressure; a pleasure
is something a sum
of suffering might annul, measurable
according to the calf on Avenue c

From the hour I was installed in happiness (now that I've given that up)
comes the time
it took my eyes or the heart to close up a picture inside

In the efficacy of a city to isolate
my old me has come now

to decrepitude but sometimes intervenes mechanically

When reality folded & appliquéd itself to us or what
we've dreamed but hiding / between 2 or 3
vesicles was the prestige

of being intangible
the nothing //
of //
a thing

If I deliver me from this (route)
excrescent, contradict(ory)
then I will sit

on my differences & sing
like the Welcome Swallows sing
around the steam grates to keep warm

to cease / light (giving it) (in order to) (give heat) / instead of (light) (lie back)

        that a diplomat's heart / be crystal / is it / transparent is it

        necessary

                      Unrobe a window to loan a new

      aspect hidden beneath the curtain /: plastic, pale, night and day // lit-up,

                      aligned // night, day

dark transparence
when I saw the fireflies over the field

    resting on the real (lie back) (lie back now)

        my voice disorchestrated over the long haul to heat a
          liquid / thinkings /

stopped my horizontal speed /
give back the line I followed my / ascensional // face

opened

all dark atoms

had left the flesh

ESSAY: *At Night the Autoportrait*

Each evening from my bed I calculated & compared
the state of my soul with the state
of Kansas, because a place also
carries a name.   Did my body make an objection to traveling
across Texas   internal conditions in which   I abstracted myself   Chicago

I never had to force myself to immigrate to the inside
thought // like a possum // playing dead // leaving as little as possible living
at a surface // which might be burned //

a lamp, a desk . . . entered the eye . . . to prove something . . . was going on . . .
     outside the skin   Baltimore

Deployed over the gutted city: an immense crude sky, scene
of some crime or other, a brusk separation   parented by nature   knowing
     nothing or understanding
nothing requires some concentration   except the things the heart can do
directly   Between the dark

& the bed approaching each place or thing my eyes
(a body) must accustom themselves anew . . . . . . If a being could be the product
     of a ground one tastes, then I was Texas developing

a vague science of joy or beauty

Forgetting the particulars that make it go

a paysage abandons a window to get an inkling
of the sky or the sky's

second elbow

NOTE: *Personal Freedoms*

I was informed that
no poems were
to be contained in
frontal
nudity. All
I was trying
to do was
write some poems. Therefore the poem
required of me that I take off
my clothes. "Because the various aspects of [humans] cause shimmering" I went out

of my way to sound like myself
in order to preserve the freedom to build statures
of oneself & whistle, because gymnastics

is exercises performed naked I demand
the freedom to watch the boys exercising in the gym, to progress

toward a more or less natural portrayal of the human body, to be fashioned
in a less or more recognizable human form to be

be given eyes that open and lips and legs that part and arms
at will Arms that stretch out to the sides and arms

and Think

and the freedom to warp the tape. You would be the one to comb your hair
over the bald spot You want science
to reveal as indicator toward the M

of a little tooth hanging all our joys
boys

on a fencepost. I demand the complete
and independent sentence
of the limbs.

ESSAY: *Noah & the Washing Machine*

To erase all color
viewed by my eyes since birth, I stared at the blue
. . . curtain . . . to operate . . . in the late . . . on the blind . . .

Denumbering thought & holding
the feathers of the wings that assimilated me

They neutralized centrifugal force by exerting contrary pressures on the subject
(that was me) to keep it
in equilibrium but not insomnia

less the humidity of earth
more the liquid mobility of light
water's goal is to accumulate light

At night: it's light that moves water, according to the eye

I sometimes saw double in time just like one sees
double in space or space
doubling

There is of course an interior
engine with nothing
reassuring about it . . . unstable, always
on the verge of busting

Meanwhile,
the photo gains a little dignity as the things that it explains are passing
from the real to the real past

It now shows me something that no longer exists

Imagine that they destroyed a park
& then they destroyed the photo

I could give you one, because this area of architecture interests me

Where we live it's just
a little piece
of cement one could
measure & count
the cracks within

A name, a date for anything
accidented by hours which later came to make the term
geology

. . . . every minute strips
of me were being . . . sheared . . . . New cells . . . regrouped . . . .

That was called: shedding my skin

a little piece in my exterritoriality

brings (blurs) to the corporal & bluets it
They folded my body into this habit:
head against the roof

a fear of folding things was soon born in me
in case the thing should wrinkle

perspective & light condensed their volume
electrical sources deafened the lights

a milky smile over the eyes   there were no surfaces
that were not mine, I got myself mixed up in a life I did not recognize, with nothing

to protect me from the mystery of ambient creatures, cabinets, peanuts; soon

the blue the room was transformed in the form
of a hive / of light / which was the form
of a prison decomposing
the colors / of light & outside

the smell of sap detached from sap

just like a shadow or shade can detach
a thread from a name

exfoliate the silk of flowers as follows:
—I accidentally opened a name pneumatically speaking, we all know knowing a name
    is a luxury exploding
    from the inside of its syllables to the outside of its ties
    I couldn't get it closed & now it no longer contains
    the name, the pleasure porch // all this that / I was sitting on

ESSAY: *The Sleepyhead*

Paysage:

a red strip of sky
compact & cutting as a band of beef jelly
over the sea already cold & blue as the fish called fish

Find gathered a rarer reunion of species as these
like the roses of Pennsylvania which hold between them petals some of the whole
trajectory of Spain or the sea sliding
on the horizontal hyphen which is the horizon sliding

Deformed swabs of clouds just outside
the center of gravity
consistency: agate; weight: visible; vapour: s

Was gravity more profound in one spot than another?

Study for the point of an eye:
when we saw the blue
prints for space or a city
in space
(*objet désagréable*)

Now they're injecting and preparing a Natural History, a writing
that no longer resembles its bizarre characters, i.e . . . my soul

will devour the intruder   When I tried
the threadwaste copper felt trick with mirrors &
added carbon at the last minute: A man

came forth, a man
appeared

holding the scaffolding up to the half-height of the sky

& then precipitating this

I made those clouds

CANTO: *Rocks (which Hold the History of the World Thus Far)*

Look! It's a rock depicting the solid
outer world! I'm looking at it through a flea-glass—It has to do

with all the human atoms in history

Live rocks are at the roots of clouds? or is it (as always) the other

way around? The grasses are a soft grace. Grasses please
the heart, rock to rock,
mountain to mount, woman

to man.   Then follows a Book
for each of the nine kinds & three faces

of rocks, beginning with Trees
& Feathers and Flowering plants.
(It goes as far as the infinite series.) First the he in here

was enthusiastic
of what and was

speaking with pebbles in his mouth, then he was running
and speaking with rocks // Next, he was a woman with salt
at the back of the throat // What conquers how we might talk
is the will to do so

There is a correspondence to the object
and a way of loos(en)ing the teeth,

                  speech,

            I sucked

the hammer & chisel from the marrow of the rock. In a pyrrhic history in the
      victory of rocks I made the ear
do the work of the eye, with a noctograph, recorded
the eidetic memory of rocks

     The dull mind rises through that which is material
     & is resurrected, anew a luminous skeleton, a thunder-,

     fire-, ice-, T.-, a bird given over
     to us newly
     tottering in new air

In rocks like unto gold or silver or stone I saw

the films of ice
the crystalline intelligence of war, still
point of the turning world, delight
taken in at the ears, the lowly
heights—Behold we are moving toward something
that resembles
a daily life (The "movies" entered in 1912); we had a done thing   a thing we had

done, & doing it   a doing thing being done & the doing of that
thing done being done   Then there were rocks. (They soon added rhythm
to speech by acquiring gestures.)   (They will add vowels and we
will express ourselves.)   Someone will cluster

consonants and we will produce pictures. (Feelings sought
refuge from absolute speech.) ("I recommend
flicking the tongue to chase out
the last of it.") Behold the beholden progressing
from past to future. Spectators jumped
from 0 to 12. Things used to be made & moved of stone
& all that was done

or felt or thought
& the myth
of all that was felt or thought and done
throughout the course of the far
forward & far back, extending
on & on in die Nacht
of rocks
& in the day
of glass
& breaking
forward & back

ESSAY: *Would Rome Be Rome*

The ensemble of signs by which we usually recognize a feeling for example love

differs between say the members of a zoophyte

Natural history shows that such

& such animal organization is

observable but a life how-

ever advanced is not. Less affirmative

are the (unguessable) states

of it through which: love

attached

not so

much to the object

for which there was a feeling of love but

to the movement toward a feeling of love to love

the object thus loved & later

to the memory of the

rage to love

the object loved i.e. What's

to hold in the globe of

say a pupil or

which part of my eye was most inhabited by me?

I am at a lost

I housed my body in the logical blank that is or was

or will be France or

fast or fat

Nominate loss

or less in the sensory case

there will always be the sediment of the unsaid in me & thank

god Can I

only live as far as I can

speak?

MY LOVE: *Odelet*

I want to say something about my love. My love is
Not where I am.
Please come in.
Breaker circuit breaker my love is
each each teaspoon in your jeans is
ever you bend down dreamy My love
is my enemy? Dummy drop
your colors, his strings rustle
in a miraculous pieces   that my love is
long & I love his long body
& its hairs. My love is
not my enemy & dummy drop
& the longest, yellowest light
He is when it hits the earth
at the longest angle, its
ankles. My love is like talking, &
evening, people, he is a tall
& tall geranium & then evening
comes before the Corinth & many birds.
My loved love taped a butterfly to a
hall a wallpaper. I did. I want to say
he is my shoulders drank from the spring
they drank from him & concurrently
riding on his shoulders from where I see
something Green, Greece, I see
everything. Then he sees the middle
of the universe which is like seeing into the center
of a piece of bread, he got burned

(because it's hot / cold there). My love, I have
a stomachache tonight & wish you were here
to scold me. My love is like talking to think
of the tall geraniums & then the sea
but I still think some things like
my love is like being thinking alone
(it's that private) I want to stand
on my love, I want to stand on his legs, I want to stand on, my
friends

MY LOVE: *More Spectacular Quadrants*

Wind, night rustles
vertebra by vertebra, building a good
    vertiginous argument

    The busy & thoughtful citizens are thinking

    in tenor of snow-
    cones, sun-
    daes—not ethnic
    cleansings in lovely
    later rhetoric. Here

    is a small island with a big
        dark beach crashing, a package
        of this far of night for you for eating

that far. It is always
    this dark. They have sent a package of black
        and white photographs of Billythekiddishness all
        gathered under the eaves and called it me
        standing at the bottom of that bundle of

    a tiny light-blue plastic keychain TV with pictures from a
    Gallery in Washington, D.C., my Fathers. Wind, night

    pops, this night's
    too cold for eating. Where is my good

love wrestling nearby to a small sparkly curve
of sidewalk which might describe

the last national square to a leaf. Will he save it? It tells the story
how a gill becomes
a lung, an ear
becomes a hair
squared. We would rather fight with words, but we fight

with these previous, precious bodies.

STUDY: *How the Palate Bones in situ Resemble the Letter L (the floor of the orbit)*

We could not see to the back of the throat. I switched on the flashlight. Nothing. The
    edge of the torrents. Glottal stop.

I have a small scar on my voice
the size of a 1-900 number I earned it
when returning from work one evening a man
I don't know made it it's composed
of seven brittle accents it's an inter-
national scar with far-
reaching origins a smoking
jacket from Tewkesbury a
psychological theory re: vice & gauze a hotel rat from Memphis Mammifer Mammiferous

What I sheltered in my voice:
a man, a woman / two men / then // several thousand of each

ARTIFACT: *When—out of . . . delight*

When—out of my *d* in the *b* of the house of *G*—the loveliness of the many-

colored stones..................,and.................,transferring that which is..........

to that which is................,.............;then it seems to me that I see myself

dwelling,................................,in some strange region.............neither......

slime......nor.........time.;and...,by the *g* of *G*, I can be t.........

—ABBÉ SUGER

ESSAY: *Seven Aspects of Milking Time*

I had it in my mind to move
my left knee toward kathenotheism or Calgary, worshiping
one god at a time

In it, the alphabet was an abolitionist

Fire was a messenger
the smoke sent up & ash. The message

: Do you want scientific replacements or creative additions : was :
: A celestial mechanics problem : How long have you been involved
   in Earth's politics

(this message is : blank) the answer is

     ever since I'm in my strong suit, my weak

     spackling the walls with bandages of light. I (may I
     say we) was

     trying to fix the place up, (we) was
     to finish the procedure, it was
     an architectural question, a spirit / spit one

       (could not)
     change cavalry to Calgary to calligram

Is each generation a further fragmentation? Was it
     Omegaville?   . . .   I think the thing is

a conquistador built of prunes & glue. The Grand Combustion

Carnival, Columbus the Cat Dancing in Flames; there are
white boys on the corner and cherry

bombs. There was only enough water to support a

an A, or a B; a boy or a   grill

There was not enough water to put out a fire
They had to import a river & kill a bunch of Black Feet. Who / I declare
a season is an agreement that hangs between heaven and here

My heroes start out in the meadowdust
& end up in the gutter

MY LOVE: *With Secret Latitudinal Knowledge*

My love and I love
each other so much we dream
the same dream of kitty litter I am not

making this up. I think we have seen
these trees before. We have crossed

a long, narrow wooden bridge swinging
toward an edge. We have passed the stoop

where each bright night another
someone is nodding out. My feet have discovered

another wave & inside is a luminous white
seal, standing up. Electrical wires in clumps

representing industrial
threats [no clean-up]. Something

disappears from the map, my loved love and I are slipping

off the twisting rope, we are
climbing back, we are not

not scared. We are

politely declining. My love and I are
happy to be here, hanging

over the crystalline wave, hanging
over the verge for a very long time.

ESSAY: *cantus infirmus*

The way to rise to god is to dissipate into particles of light like
you can rise in the water from an ion and in "The Rise
of Sex Towards God" a hard-on is another
anagogic approach And adopted into the family
of King
& I the beggar whom the strong hand has lifted
manifested by twofold swallows smallness malls
my name in sugar the King
of France
was my
father
sister
the bestiary abbey
at St. Denis my mother, my name
in sugar the King
of Crows
cranks
the eukaryotic
cypress King my
mother
King
of jelly kelp sugar my
mother feather King
of smallness & con
-strained
two times
by smallness & king of
ex-cons king kong pebbles & small of family King
Philip Came Over From Great Spain for Kingdoms phylum class (subclass)

order (suborder) family genus species Chordata Vertebrata Mammalia
Eutheria Primate Anthropoidea Hominidae Homo We're all binomial in the
typological species concept of classifying, so hello phylogeny & confident to
martyr mater KING manifested by twofold smallness swallow KING

& on the giant glow-ball to be interpreted later
giant Ys inscribed in strings of light on the face of the earth

ORIGINS: *My Life in Moving Pictures*

If I'm a leaf I'm a leaf If you're a
tree I'm illegitimate

I remember the very day I discovered it
(yesterday)

A PLAY:

(My father plays the part of the speaker. If the father is not available, anyone
will do—hang this sign around the actor's neck: The Author's Father)
(curtains)

Hello, Birds. Birds! Hello!

(Birds "have little to say")

Birds! I say! Are you having a
party, birds?

(Here, the camera records several bird subjects through
the reeds, the reeds bob with their weight & deafening
twitter)

BIRDS!

(Birds are noisy among the weeds, above
the marsh, red-winged blackbirds are,
but do not answer)

Birds! Vultures with metacarpals
built like trusses on aircrafts & bridges, birds with certain
wing-load-to-weight ratios, birds who carry
booty in their beaks & birds Black-capped & air that allows them
Blue-footed, iridescent of the head, slipping through, Herons with
sleeking feathers, who's your father, who? Birds, "My question, answer

in the fewest words,
what sort of life is it
among the children
of the birds?

ESSAY: *In the World that was Slated to Be Reapportioned that Day or This*

I had a crisis in my male domesticity
without being more than someone // or someone // else

my little personal police exploding
the envelope of all things
chrysanthemum or me

To the so-&-so I carry inside my bonnet:
my head's not near it

renouncing the diplomacy of all thought or not (requires)
an amulet against // belief // in danger // preserves me
thus
love radiate out toward the thing
loved finds there
an impassible
surface & ricochet

I didn't dare disturb a parcel
that love doesn't carry the lover's name
I am not in a hurry to renew pain I don't
understand very well what it is I ask
I realized a way to kill a love I was not
courageous enough //

I tried to fray the bed as softly as possible
with rustlings, with leaves. He

was reading a book. There was a man // on television saying

prayers, saying

just a little more

possession of just a little more

man // or // woman. I had thought that would not be possible. Now, I see it's not

difficult at all.

SKETCH: *Episode B at Gold City*

As an aid
for apprehending the vanishing point:

*(line drawing here of two
torsos in waves, 11' x 8')*

Here is my
difficulting diffusing grace (lux

gratiae) in the mouth
of space & light

an empty open window through
which I view that which will be
painted there

in the walk from the walk
to the window, sound

flew in splinters across the square for "the
good things on earth" Lundis and luz

I was baptized in the symphony of fast, slow, fast, slow slow

My eyelids separated cities, with maps which moved
through fluids in heads, maps are displaced

street by street when I return to that place

ordinary light is replaced
glass is replaced (with magnets)
the human eye is replaced (with a fluorescent screen)

among the first things seen were
butter, transformers

among the fast things
you

ESSAY: *On the First Lines of the Invocation to Light*

(Now we will speak of)

the various parties which made up the particles
of the sunset I never saw or Was it
the religious representation of it—
The sun: stiff—geometric—stigmatized—a miraculous sign(ing).

I must have thought that each minute was just a choice of paintings (arbitrary
enough) that one had before one's eyes with no relationship to the place it depicted.
This one was a subway scene in which I found myself with strangers and that one
had a background of trees, grass, green. Another was a situation in which
somebody told me to do something & I did it & eventually they gave me money, though
it was never enough. I was soon able to distinguish materials if not forms.

Now I'm looking at the Study on Clouds executed
in blue & put under glass which is of course
the Atmosphere. What
would be capable of putting profundity behind the color
of things? Soon
I'll study the longer days
like those at the poles that night interrupts but
for a minute.

To be noted later:
What good *is* a brain

ESSAY: *The Complete Sentence of the Limbs*

I was bathing as an individual in something more general
with my habitual gestures of face & eyes

I interrogated the window Did you
see him or him or her ? Did you see // the sky?

A woman melted
into the ground of several
women & a man left over from the
old war which they repolished to make it
look new again (world #3) The amber piece of the
it said: Here // are your dead The glowing
fragments . . .

When I think of you I thought of you in waves // of color
but not grain // An enemy
dream forced its way
into (my) sleep

There were so many forms I / they hadn't yet isolated
in / from the vast spectacle viz. reality
Light invented new solids like light

on the surface of a lake. There were
certain forms that favored me—the
flattered & unstitched river, . . . arms, legs.

Afternoon I was an empty
being [bed], no weight. Now look: They've given me <u>this</u>
The weight of my re-made self weighs
as much as dinner   So much
do things in general tend to want to continue Sleep
is a forcible narcotic   difficult to deflect

I only employed urban terms for the sea & for the city maritime verbs for the sea.
    Yesterday

there was an indication of the richness of the material my
feet made contact with: Bending
knees, buckling legs. It was called

the nervous present

No one resembles a straight road but this one had a few more curves
than usual. Will, belief, & sentiment formed
a tangled sediment around my skirts

It's the other parts of myself that follow the other
parts of me Is that will to be green or
gray-green ? If my will had given my (eyes) another
address (reorganizing atoms into contraries) I
an interior interview with a series
of yous in huge attitude

Ideas continued to flower one adding itself to another as
the old ones left deafly or a memory does but leaf-deaf The human you see before
you represents a victory / (over adolescence, banality, howling terms, barbarity)

Certain details detached themselves
from their duties and floated away A coffee cup became a saucer Few
noticed Women & men on whom the flesh still works A mass
of ductile material Existence has little interest except in days &
dust but the dust
is magic (works like a magnet) Whatever

it is or was or are, the somethings inhabiting surfaces of bodies which I
will soon dress to make presentable I have this to say

My mobile is   not virtue
but I try to

I have a book linked to my fragile brain but the lines are hard
to see It could
drop off at any minute or it may
begin to write itself tomorrow—
these exact minutes right this very one are the ones
of all my life that I love best & am
glued to

or you

heard the grinding of my nerves independent of exterior objects which can some-
times mislead a nerve And I complained a little for all the neighbors because I

sensed they could not see their tables // were planets but
could sense
their troubles

Flocking

to the flavor
of the neighbor at dinner
won't help it   Atoms like people will open
& often regain their density

& make an exit exist in a nothing which was everything

I would now like to show "the brilliant stain" that you are
moving across the fields or through the street your profession
appears as a professional human detaches
from you "a brilliant
stain moving"

so many you can't tell where the horizon sea etc.
All

my animals pebbles candles feathers
I will have to sleep a long time to find them again

ESSAY: *For Anyone Who's Ever Sped Apart*

What symmetry can there be
between a nation & a dog? dusk
& a candle? a corolla & this road?

Build you in her loveliest (Iowa)
Acknowledge you her head (in Kentucky)
& guard angelic guard (New York)
Irradiate civic with virtual
touch / trash (on landfill).

In the anatomy
of anatomy (hand torn from leg), in the very red that brights, this blood
falls out of emotions, and makes each pretty artery in this body   a resting leaves.

Among these,
I remember I loved you
as if you were dead, arm torn
from armament, headless

from head; so fit my hands
in pairs, leg with legs, hands
with birds manifest and the melody
of them. Speeding

from a head or a heart birds
unpack the works, birds I may
obey, symmetrical birds in my virtuest birds I might
in pursuit of roads and balance, birds.

ESSAY: *Who Thinking on her Legs (Manifesto)*

What color is your arrow? Mine is
green.

I'm the nail & you're the nurse

I walk across the street & you
pull the thorn You mail it

to me. You try to steal my reader
& you succeed & then you steal my dress.

You are as unable as any lioness to sell thickets back to forests, I
am a blind f-line

You are trying to be culturally specific o.k.

I am every effort of the self
to describe the self, you are falling

deaf on deaf ears, but everyone's watching (TV). This is no
attempt to insist that flux

can know flux but you
flex your muscle and mine (!) I am exoplanets & you are extrasolar o.k., how far a ray

of light can go from the beginning of time to I am other places

where night follows day like Cicero
said I'd rather know myself than Don

145

King You are the spectroscopic method & changes starlit
frequency vs. I'm the astrometric method
in the coliseum artifacts of Telescope, o.k.

You stepped in velvet on your way to the studio, I was never a professional
exam-
iner of Kansas

I was running neck & nekid with

smoke & smoke
could be said to be loose too; You

are artichokes you are butter & seeds & you can
hit a homer, therefore you can hit a home run

You are America Someone Someone is an encyclopedia of computer tears
I was 5

you were 3
I had a closet & hid there, you
walked out of it

You were the disposition to think together with the discovery
of iron & wheat & what
created private property, primary colors, war, this need
for success I'm public property, I am aiming this
at your voice

ESSAY: *Of Sun, Of History, Of Seeing*

In this one, seeing is a form of touching
(take darsan / take image / take sight)

the eyes are the last part completed
the eyes are finally opened with a golden needle

At the moment of its most complete
irradiation : the navel : the eye : unfolds
a (silk)
pavilion

a
peduncle
of

(gold)

leafing
into the road the goal

becomes
to obey (without
question)

the (something)

linked by way of
(something)

to an hour
a season
with nothing

in particular
to justify it —

as hard as I tried   /   a screen of my eyes
to have nothing   in front of them   but my hands

as in when looking one is said to see
the thing better when looking

away //

to adhere to there /

I couldn't ankle the effort of other flowers to satisfy

the names which came to faces to make
a person : the eyes are finally opened with a golden needle

to answer the luminosity of creation with simple organs

I shall survive on prairie mice

EPISTLE: *Dear Maximus, Dear Reformer*

Dear

Do I really have to become familiar with the ways race
and class inform cinematic representations of relations
between the sexes? I am looking at a man
on the train at dawn. He is wearing a Red
uniform and I am only interested in him
as a representative of the uniformed species. The train
pulls in underground. He crosses his ankles
when a church goes by. And when we come
out—Oh, I am sorry, you will have to wait until
another history, when short butt cracks have come back
into favor. I / she had never contemplated the length of
butt cracks till she met him / you. Before
I met him I never thought about butt cracks, this
is my testimony. I now know he needs a quarter, so he can hide it
in there, along with the American movies.

ARTIFACT: *The Alphabet Caliphs (ABCs)*

of the

"Be and it was"—

of the

The Bestower of

(Of Colors). Of the

variegated workshop, the Portrait- . . . of . . . has painted with the

pen of (His) . . . clemency, the . . . . in the most . . .

in accordance with . . . . . . "And he has . . . . and he has

. . . . . . daybreak . . . . . . bread . . . . . . dirge of the dead . . . . . . the Field of
      Reeds, a carnelian bowl

of honey . . . . discord drags a dog, thunder . . . and he

has . . . he has . . . stylus stick spatula brush, a bowl of lapis lazuli

filled with butter . . . he has . . . what the eye requires : : stepped into her bright

chair . . . . . . he has what color was the light

in your window; . . . . . . graffiti in the master's

mature halo : he has : animate inanimate

. . . a body draped . . . in the skin of beasts . . . he has . . . under the covers

darkness, water . . . he has . . . over the covers, ... has sky with white

holes, has . . . . . . let the earth bring forth and creeping thing he has and every
      herb before it and

she has hammers unencumbered, she has . . . and she has . . .

"magnesium flares and shoes and [he has] hoes"

—KHWANDAMIR

TRAVELOGUE: *When We Consider the Dark Light*

if you could hear a town grow, to wonder about other, distant objects
by the 10s and dozens   a block away   from everything   in the world:

(saw them) in Ontario hauling tobacco up to the rafters, Erie Eau town
to the right, & to the left, the Erie Eau girls

I lay flat of my belly (this is an old hobo trick) washing my feet
in Niagara water   To the left, the stretch into endless
are dark at night"   the incalculable

is a vast number
increased by multiples, then by squares

the length of one zero
occupies how much space

it takes
me to wake

the body
as a boat

which crosses
death   or sleep   is it with

or without
measurement?   the "heart" is the seat

of the "intellect"; the heart is wrapped in paper & re-inserted; the head
takes animal form (*qubehsenuf*)   probably

a cow, just as a man or woman will smoke the lights
moving in and out
at the darkened peripheries

of cities or an atom's parts
will weave at the brightish middle, and when we

put our fingers to the heart,
it goes out, lighting it up

by thinking the thinking heart   so smokeable

MY LOVE: *Music Does*

Music is a dog
that sleeps & lies & my
love lies down
with me my
true love lies
down, & he too
does possess
the capacity
for speech
& he speaks
to me he
says my true
love lies
down
with me hmm. What doesn't
my true

love like? Lilies. S/he

loves them. Now
she's lying on the table of Ls, his

love looming
in available sunlight. His thinking thinks sunlight
and, why won't she

eat the bitter
dandelion green, hmm, we are building a house
on a catalpa flower.

ESSAY: *The Infinite Assonances Within*

The New York phone book is suggestive of a sublime
genius, beyond human origin, a domesticated list
of names drawn in much
as an evil spirit will be drawn & contained within
a small, blue safety bottle. Here are heroes and djinns. We are drawn
not to its contents but to its mystery. It should be microminiaturized
by hand & worn
on a chain around the neck, an Ifrit in a cucurbit, to touch upon
delicate, upon agile & dexterous,

a light field ergonomically created at night, a theory
of the means of the process of the toucher who touches upon
names, a field lightly. The names
escape in a black cloud of naming. And if it were graven

in the eye corners it were a warner
to those who would be warned
at that corner or this:

when the index has power enough
to weigh down atomic factors, the tactile corpuscles take
advantage when the touching is touching
upon a field restrained within the adjacent names which harness

the possibilities of flesh and spirit properties, anatomophysiological practicalities
of famous violin players' brains; what is contained

within the touching finger? the little pinky
is not irrelevant, nothing

is. The total of names does not point to the souls of this city
or to the distance between bodies but
rhymes Hence hey everybody is

those that touch
the ones they're touching & she who touches
upon a thing dark or light might read us thus
What is happening anywhere, what has happened, and what will

ARTIFACT: *Two Ink on Pottery Fragments
(7th–8th c. A.D.)*

Ostracon, 1

. . . Behold, another 4
carrots I gave . . . If he desires that I lay upon them [   ] then he thinks that
[   ] a large [carrot] is a large [   ] it is a large . . . turnip [   ] until
dinner, and I shall give it [   ] Tell these matters to all the peas.

Ostracon, 2

Farewell in the L. Give it
to him, the whole, the . . . the
humblest   of all sliding
vegetable dish

the radishes lit up like minor
fireworks out on the river

ESSAY: *The Alien & Beautiful Light of Waking, Rain, Night*

At evening

announced on flight

Sign to stray light
Signs to stray light!

Sign to siren to signal

Siren to signal, signal to stray light

The flight goes

     down & up, side, under, maybe

To paradise   a port

As a sea so over

hurrying toward wheels, Sunday

before we must get up, rise, dress to seem

presentable, brush teeth, train, hurry, truck, work, the flight

     the lull, heave, phosphor
       change, the

                    birds
fall down, everyone

          to sleep, another

clock-related gene, time-
less . . . . . . light . . . acting upon time . . . . . . a beautiful oscillation

in RNA cycles. Here is the discontinuous logic of sleep, in which
the answer to the question "What is sleep for?" is
"Because we sleep," disgorging

                 rise, dress, fly, eat

The white space represents light, and light . . .
is waking

             dressing, work

I hope these connections are clear:

the metal silts
flame cell & metal salts clot
arcs between carbons
candle flame & a sodium light are examples; brace-bounded; I can't tell the melody
for the plot

          The plot is: rise, eat, sleep

          The melody:

the fever that fret air my
melody melody fret   the snaffle briedel, light slips
stops to measure sugar, Brix

& sugar cubes under our pillows in case
we got hungry at night. That's all
there was before the war & after the war there was war & before the war
He worked in a sugar factory My
father did, died. Night

prepares the cells

for "Hot, Cold, Moist, & Dry":
atom A, atom B, atom C fight to make:

to make or unmake new grains (silicon + O_2)

or in the emptier waste, resembling air

He fell from night to dawn, from dawn
to day to noon from noon to night he
fell. Who? My father.
Is a drunk & fell.

a satin spar in my
heel god

of course
is tyrannical, but what
made me dark was

[love]

while night invests

eld things, night
prepares the cells

My father fell.

He was nearly blind & she was nearly
deaf—who? My
eyes my head hath darkness of dark
thing my soul I said

has devoured the intruders for I have inherited the ABCs & the Pill

(Even as a child the sound of machinery was the enemy)

I am not in the image but my voice was. I am
with my voice, I come with it

just like this stereo comes
with speakers by which to hear you by.
Hear you? Hello.

[the heel is lifted, head is turned, arm raised]

Here is your good news
your inspired cryptogram
depicting the decline of practically everything
This garment made of skins is a noble possession
& will soon get me arrested
the Naked House of Nakedness, where you stand
in order to speak out "otherly" as
"Allegory" when clothed—. i.e. I had shoes, I had shirts. Did I

see an acacia in the desert   *Homeridae*
Did I drink?
Did this stereo speak?
I had my right name, was
rectified. Did they
address words to me?
I was involved in what was dissolved in the process
[cells]. You are

Zoonomia.
The Father Question:

Father fell. Is the reverse
also true? Can the inverse
be deployed   destroyed?

Periods of time, hurry back
to ice, to fire, to find

and found no end
& then again
& find no end either but
no beginning

    rise, sleep, eat eat rise sleep sleep

  we riseth sleepeth eateth & wotteth not whither . . . till break
  of day . . . & she cometh . . . & she burneth . . . awaketh I theth theth

& fear not boys with bugs

For I have gathered frogs
and I have gathered dirt
and I have gathered
and I have gathered weeds
and I have gathered wood

The age therefore of the universe was a man my father falling

The figure falls short
at the globular star clusters the figure falls
& counts the parts. & picks pearls apart
The parts: 1H 2O 4S
no one wants a universe
younger than its parts

Send these atoms back immediately!

c/o I'm afraid I'm hungry I'm happy I'm fearful I love you To bite you I'm sorrow for your Ha in the face of Ha Ha I'm the force with which

a body   moves
against resistance.   What

body?

Catalyst:

of discrete agencies I wish to
produce a more effective result
than the sum of the results produced
by the same agencies acting independently; I am as two drugs for example human
will & holy spit, I am the sum of the cooperative action of two or more organs of
the human body, I am a word that has the same meaning, or the same general
meaning, as a particular word, I am a more or less satisfactory equivalent for it, as,
I am "joyful," I am "glad," I am "happy," "elated," I am "pastoral simplicity" and
"contentment," I am "arcadia," I am an alternative but less approved science, I am as
a species or a genus

New hydrogen atoms are correctly made
in the interstices
of space as space

itself expands

It's not my head that hurts
but what's inside it

What's inside it?

    They say conscience was installed as a smoke

        detector later

        The age therefore of the universe was a woman
falling

        The plane
        falls, birds, rain
        The rain

in Spain & in Puerto Rico

the rain it raineth in Goleta & in Island View

it raineth in Los Angeles & at Dundalk

radiant radiant rain

HISTORIES: *The Great Handiwork (Water, & Soft, Delicious Air)*

All of them the great . . . mmm . . . did
establish . . . . . . and so divide
mmm from me. So, too,
the earth was bounded by water, & the
boots to walk on to fit the river, the
transit of whole cities to heaven. Don't sleep at night solidly
as clearly night is possible. It is also possible
in a physical sense: earth was objective & dark,
floating on water. As with
the eclipse, so the conflict of water. Moistness of seeds,
semen, so we go
floating between vapor & liquid, solid, the highest
apple on the happy branch we wanted to reach

If of apple or
if of air, come,
take.

HISTORIES: *The Pots & Pans of Early Greece*

The pots & pans
of early
Greece were really
breakable, red-
figured, black, silhouettes banging
around Herakles'
knees; but even He
was "more than a woman," circa 1973
in the spirit of '76 to get
out, busting moves on the well-lit dance floor, who learned his letters
from the fertile crescent, to call Anaximander's "something"
energy. We were . . . of all that happened
in the *petite patrie* of Sophocles—boys under the sheets
with their mothers. Parmenides
suggested where to hook faith in the mouth, that substance
of things looked for
but not received, hectic & reeling
into the centuries' sleep. Heraclitus

looked at the same world and came
to other conclusions, like Strife, when the
never-ending fire seems to strike
the strobe light dead, twice. This is the story of our reckless
lineage, the beginning of the road we trod in the
brotherhood of beings of primeval days, a
collapsible House of Origins appearing from its palace-
prison, a human ghost loved in the shape of a swan under the heights

HISTORIES: *The Flesh*

Living in the lap
of lux-
ury
& sleeping sleep I will
arrive in this poem
to corinthianize
on all your native sleepless settlements
who cannot dig
a canal through rock even
with a golden
pick shovel Nero

also wanted to redesign the heart
of the hydrogen
bomb It's like adjusting the quills
on a hedgehog (useless) & to ill
goods, heroes, subway riders, away! teachers teaching
chemistry in the South
Bronx do not
stand up for it; hear
music in the way the hounds
race through the woods; ex-
animate the factory, the flush

HISTORIES: *A Woman Was Constructed in 20 oz. Antiquity, Certainly She Existed*

It is true that [   ] discovered the
clitoris in 1544, key
to heaven and
hell, viewable

to the naked eye, like

a man in the forest, or birds,
they spoke   [latin]

"I itted it." "What
did you it?" "That," he
said, pointing.   The body

is a well-oiled
machine, made

for doing things. I forgot

what I can do, she said,
talking talking   She has taken the care
to change her necklace for the domination
of anyone, a female

revolutionary all jellied into action, a
living organism with sizzling

feelings.   Right in the middle of something really
beautiful happening, "your frontal
lobes are scraped out with a nail file"

The beautiful thing that was
happening was happening between us; it was

the highest friable branch of the apple, like a glass
chassis in the glove of a chandelier

HISTORIES: *That Wobble of Light*

I hereby cluster all day loveliness with flick
off a switch and weigh the earth, scraping
our baffled feet on sandpits of fleas
to dance. For I
said I saw a flea circus today and understood
a small planet and 20 billion frames
of families of a truth divine lording it over
the ghosts of material things which accompany human
bodies.   Love walks

softly across
the surfaces, maybe of the house. The three great works of the Samians include
a 1,100-foot tunnel dug by hand under 900 rock feet. When humans finally
destroy that rock what will happen to under the after-
world's altar when presidents were pretty, porridges grand, a mole
in the sea built nearly 120 feet deep?
& in our clothes we walked on golden streets
which house and unhouse as many men & women as birds
with feathers so sharp they wound.   Values?

Ecclesiastes subjects, I will shoot you
through the heart, Minneapolis, in my ideal country
if my hands are cold I do not build
a fire of your house.

HISTORIES: *Birth, without the Theme of Burning (Us, born of a thicket)*

Then all the forests divided & them oceans &
overwhelmed this finite wall of flesh
shut up in infinite revolutions
& elevated on the human neck. The head
is the hero here—I mean the brain
groveling along Bond Street, through Tompkins
Square, while in lead suits the inhabitants
of suburbs walk heavy: soft & bent are the bones
of citizens who weep & greet them
ending forests at the door. Be not as the swan
invented for decoration on lakes divided, *Homo cosmicus,* come forth
to witness the night from Mona Kea, exploding
1,000-year old rockets and all
our millions of chemicals inside us, resting now. The absolute speed

limit is night, no one
invented it, not law,
not physics. O winter
desires I wonder
under cool eaves, should we really be eating
frogs? fishes? rabbits?
lobsters? sweetmeats?

ESSAY: *An Amateur of Human Ichthyology*
(hairshirt woven in #s) (I could only brush the enve-
lope without touching the contents at all)

I hear person from a practicable point of view
but when nature introduces a person into a body, she shouldn't
mutilate the flesh so much

to add a ravishing shoulder to the mix // inalterably material for a minute

form's indecision is reflected
by hair breaking into dusk

the tortures a beautiful
body performs on its beautiful legs, arms, cells, neck, etc.

the polish of the flesh
imposes itself between me, forced into the role
of guarantor of the tooth, a public

disturbance, an epistolary
noise to wake the dead; Dear Head,

I know you are no longer yourself

I am not writing to who you are now, but to who you will be
when you are no longer yourself again, yielding

innovator of a knot re-inquarked, the secret

with which each inside life escapes from itself, gilds
itself and returns at the spaces aiming
at the human-to-be-made: an alphabet collar of hairs, woven in white

ODE: *To My Peoplery, Little Trees*

Nothing binds
a community like cats catching flies
like spending money at the corner store
money binds many birds
a community, handing out cigarettes
lighting matches with shaky hands
soda pop binds, and wine   There are no
trees here oh no, no trees
diminishing trees I miss you
where did you go in the crystal dark, disappearing
into Brooklyn's arches like an infinity   infidelities   untrivial trees tippling

over secretly into when no telephone poles exist, satellites orbing, toppling into
radar sound when no one was watching barely-there trees
birth little trees, have a little nose, are hiding
in the sidewalks of this city   They
please help the consequent trees trying to get more significant
eat cigarette butts, drink wine, have big eyeballs
So there they are in their jackets
"Someone should open a way for them through the ice"

                    Trees
                            think of snow
                    They
                            know duration

The Russians are not apologizing to them
The Mexicans are burning them

The Americans—there are no
good Americans

There is an invisible tree
in your pocket, your book or in your purse, it's invincible
Trees still do
a newspaper or two.
There are ghost trees in your subway and buslines, at Bergen Street,
plus real trees at the green pit that is Morningside Park

No, that's a python, this is a bog with trees beyond the Pillars of Hercules
In the laws of less-and-less, trees confine to one sex what
in humans can profitably be done by two Who-
            soever has been initiated into the mysteries
      of Kabeiri knows what I mean:

                  O thou thouest of trees' throat and frogs forsake being for sale

unto saplings; trees, like movies and dinosaurs their bodies are getting bigger
      their brains, small

Smaller, you are sitting on a chair that used to be a tree   I cannot explain this
      as metonymy

        the eyes of my people, so those on stars
        of trees, trees
        What you breathe!

Maiden doctor fix this tree
its chichis and choners

moghuls and trees. Gen
                    X is

              better than trees. dead fishes
          in dead seas
          tanks of everything poison! I banish you from rivers and trees for I feel
all hysterical for trees.
The Niger gum's tired, "la woods" is

another way to say "little tree" traveling with stars in a
folding landscape, falling R
yea deep in paralysis the blue goal is no howlitzer, Gum Shoe,
              abuse the scene
              by rotting a weed
              in it: you is
              the weed. No, no
              it's me, a
              minor tree, her
how early around the ears, There was
a tiny tree. All she heard was inserted
On that scaffolding, with the aid of ropes, infinitesimal trees
move up and down the faces of buildings

CITIES: *The Last Lights off the West*

In darkness   a paperweight
   on the twilight hum of
      hum.   A whole
           paper-built world; all the little details rendered
         in holepunch and pinking shears.   Thus opens that setting.

(And) I laugh in the face of poprocks
& bottle rockets   Nelson who got
three fingers blown off   But he was just a kid   Not a kid
from my American past but a kid just the same,

     whole ships with

clouded leopards in the hold going down
mid-sea.

This is before farming and the rise
of great cities,   the first dividends
of culture, the facts divide   before

the junior-sized dehydrated
city with missing women and children. Just add water
to the bite-sized city built

upon all of its histories, trilobite
and manhole cover. Nelson
the astronomical signs in three fingers
of DNA. Gold-coated casts
of the first cut marks ever. That is how

we build and end each disturbed paper backdrop in this city. And set it
aflame. Extreme regions
of the heart shut up
within them-
selves all other countries—Where
are these?   (Curtains.)

CITIES: *From the Edge of Prospect*

Realize that I believe
Enormous
is a large amount of money
Enormous will pay the rent and
   buy a dog stuff.

     All day I was distracted by blue, lead-

able as dead
blue reluctant to turn

right that leads not
where blue but
buildings halo it, also clouds,
gray, crowding, ready

to rain, crowded people. People with their private feelings early
in the morning. That one thinks

she can't carry all her gold with her, so she takes it
little by little on the bus in a city "drifting steadily
     toward ruin," other cities drift
       slowly toward night, filling

with human bodies and
their stuff. I can't

pretend it doesn't matter that some
people suffer everywhere, that everywhere

some do. There will be clouds
for the sky not
as symbol for half the

world. There will be that happy star when fear
enters the heart at hearing, then above

so below will I ride my necks till rejected, with a cry to my
tribe, water
has been found! . . . Meanwhile, at the mall, no winged

victory except if
a tennis shoe, no David but
atop the station wagon. And had we
rolled on the stunning ground   and had we walked
out of a country

built of "enough," had a grace come
in the form of a pea Waiting
for a taxi she stitches up
enormous holes

in the social fabric, The one Brown one Blue
eye

of humanity. Cool
dust in the lungs. For those who come

for cake and lemons, give them cake &

lemon, heaven, & no tax for evening, no
tax for daybreak, & no thing more than enough

Night (They're putting the winds
back in their cages) & they

are always present They
are always doing something unpleasant

to me or my friends, this is why I hate
poetry, and I quote: "the traffic sounds like gods"
"as if the lilacs martyred themselves" "fire-drowning" in speech
Now it's time to clear some throats

& break the poet's bones All the prices
on all the sonnets
like a boxer's tower along "the warm resources of my mouth"

Trees stay outside
Words do

Believe that I think that light

at the end of the tunnel is not
the end of the tunnel but

trains   Where did I get
the Cloud of Unknowing,   Golden

Parachute woven in advance? Oh,
pigeon! stop! I stands there & shout

CITIES: *The Raggedness that Drives this Limb*

The wind has "blown it away : grammar."
If the wind blows it away, you
can see it : my stilts, struts, my clouds

                  puffed up
          like buffalos, buffalos like
            clouds floating
               across the
               field or silty
                    sky from
                   which the
         mind pulls down

        dark out of a
               glove
box loving

twenty days in two afternoons. Twenty days in forty. A plethora
of afternoons; a dirge; as many
fill a winter. Forget about grammar; think

closely of how
winter is a folder
to look back in the way
we came or
accordion
out; a siren

spinning its bright

tires

in the

winter

noise like ice spinning

from the sky, since it reinvented diamonds

of ice tonight, raining, and the siren must get somewhere. The obstacles

of animals and this

part of the cliff; we drive across

the high pale

earth surrounded, what

is a tense : to struggle.

CITIES: *Trains*

She's fine till work lets out
  then the conversation begins,
    the many bags, wheel-heavy rumblings,
                  cardinal questions
    A cardboard box some-
      where, the "lower versions
      of cities / flattened under"
    her watery feet. She crosses the river
   in a flowered skirt. She is floating, "flawless and dead."
The hood of her sweatshirt spreads
  out across the ears, the
whole crowned head.

    A seagull
  peels back, a little gray sky
   in its wing & the sky, gray
  on top of the river below such a

How many bridges did you take?
  Two. I made two.
  But Queens is still
   on this island

If I ever accidentally left
all my books if I ever
left my body
        in Queens, Long Island

      to see columns of Queens
      to paint columns of Queens

         5 minutes of furry heart
         5 minutes of furry heart

      you can't tell the difference
but one's a furry valentine-shaped
                 heart
The other is human

CITIES: *Bringing Forth a New Impression of Youth & Charm*

Look at the bright surface (the eye
superficially surveys) below

: the pink skies of New Jersey:

They turned up the underground & concocted
crude works. Hidden veins digged up & boiled
to blackest grain;   If I ever did get lost

in New Jersey

or if they ever got rid of New Jersey
just ripped up all the elements, nipples of Jersey
City, Paterson, if we left it
alone for a few
minutes & all the trees
grew back
and covered the Earth with Days Inn
with Shoprite peanutbutter my hair who beholds this bright
surface etherous
mold which we were dirty
I just want to go back to New Jersey
& win eleven thousand five hundred daily
because I saw a small room a moon there
over the freeway billboard at seven p.m.

CITIES: *Above My Ordinary Train*

I feel gone from going where I go. Where I
went. I went again. Where did I
go? Anywhere

a skyline did.

A skyline dims
over the skyline below

below which are spires, dogs, sparkly
sidewalks, rivers to be glinting, and other

gutters without water, pigeons in clusters—and other
other things. In this city of unsimilars I give my body

to science
and mosquitoes, but I still want to live in it
despite

carhorns & reckless
poverty, all forms of carbon
copies, hard-ons, declining
trees & me

& my organs to you, Carlotta.

CATALOGUE: *And Why for Poetry Like Life is "Exquisite in its Kind"*

(INTRODUCTION)
I observe how imperfectly words
preserve, therefore, as one should not grow more corn
than one can get in, I shall live no more than I can record

(BODY)
thoughts specified and a number of thoughts un–,

in a riverfront town, hipness is produced by dissolving present into future,
past into p.,

through hand-waving and grocery lists, stone-throwing and stones, a totaled
number of minutes looking from kitchen window where there were grasses.
There was a tarp, a trap, little crocuses. There was purple, yellow, and white

(OF ALL POSSIBLE CONCLUSIONS)
a "shone," a
"came alive," all I'll carry
inside my head, the death of
O, birds & the book
in my hand, the high philosophy (ferocity) I'll follow, of wolves and bears

ESSAY: *Of Cannibals, Of Thumbs*

what revolves in the thinking disk? what reflects of the eye is due

not only to its material composition but also

to the shadows of ideas one is making based on peoples places taken

in. E.g., a field a floor a pair of hands rubbing themselves & nimbused

by a door. Forgetting under the image or the thing

was the hollow as expressed in the shadow

beneath the thumb. It was little more

than the minutes each which I am burning to cover. Each which one

stretched out in front. Until this moment my life

continues to cease

to collect my total life. Offered is a possible

multiplication of my me—That is,

joy. Joy, multiplied, begets

joy. Joy taken

in begets

it; that is, joy, rubbing

itself, joy

based

on it, its own ideas, joy on the floor

rolling in the minutes devouring

itself its material composition its mineral and crystal tears, joy stretched out and I

am burning,

burning to cover joy's shadow of joy beneath the thumb.

ESSAY: *The Hanging Paradogs Slip*

There is an octave between us.

Plus money-movements and the painfully plain
rose, a martyr eaten by dogs, with thumbscrews, acony, and one

sawn asunder; Let's take off our clothes. Life at the heart
is not yet arranged
at the surface. Here is a bankruptcy: dealing with bone
& marrow, husbands & white of things
nearest & next in this
dangling barrel, a booklet for the Carolines reflecting the mystery of I can't what

kind of flower, the devil

's head, people,   as we do, crammed
into the wall

    That his hands   that he is
      in thoughts,   before killing it
   into   meat, that he is
no, friends, he is

the feeling of saying something in the parking lot   He is Sears and the towers
know that I could never be sleeping of English sleep with failing
                    beatitude on top of Macy's   with a name that never
does not point, but hangs
in a heavens of letters, ravens

rat-star, sugar. Apertures
of beetles & stumps
cupola of midges, oh blisters! oh you! [aside: I leave the little scaramouch
alone in all his glory] Good-bye, cornstarch! Good-bye! vanity!
    Appellations! Good-bye,
"Fire!" Aunt Mary, carpets of atmosphere & debilitated
retina in the bland
atmosphere land, c. 1973, when I first came into consciousness. I could see the city
below us laid out like a distant watering hole only

when he doesn't drink it, as I once did
    derive   from goods and pleasures. So many parts missing, yet I will have my full sip
of wine &
peaches later. I regain one by one

one hand, foot, finger, heart, my thought. My thought standing
walking, working out, there, out on the water! Look, where I will it,
I see it! leaping from roofs! Good-bye! And return my head
to the sea; and the sound
of the waters, reflecting steps
into the river, and the colors, cloud
the voice of the man
woman as at any moment in the vast
past now Dissemble
the elevator to speak with the surfaces of wolves I will not talk
to this you, you take it

FILM: *How to Exploit an Egg*

from the material body or the material
that makes up a body (textiles, dry goods)
or the materials from an

egg including nitrogen &
I want to make a green

film in which
Clytemnestra comes back
& an egg is divided
into sun, & a moon
which spreads
over the sky like

whites and in the
patates of patates in the
myth of the rape
of potatoes I would put

a woman
back in the sky, a woman
dancing in a mask made by Eleni
on a screen of gray which is a blue

film of the myth
of all Sisyphus. She is dancing on the small
cubits
of microspace
which make up the rocks

—Wherefore speak you so, Stranger?

—Is it me you mean?

—It is you I mean, I mean you, Stranger
    voice voicing the material body in shiny anterooms

Moon, O moon, hearken
& reflect: this egg-house made to birth surfaces liquid & curved

Said egg, come, mock rock & bone
come, skull, shell, hull formed inside
come, ship, brains, & beans
o, come, paw, dabble & dangle in sugar pools
Said curved egg, come, claw
come, cigars sent by lords
come, liver, come fur, be birthed
& bent space itself will truly think in every limb & velocity of stars

SONG: *King Paradise Who Sharpens a Dog's Tooth*

What is and /or are me and /or is /are not me speaking
on the green-spot which is
paradise? Paradise is a pea. A p. is a person. A paradise is a
probe in the ear, an atomic force
microscope; and in the ear is the sea's
buoy—what the organ
of corti contains: a man aflame.

The big room in New York is getting empty now
It's just an old rag with a big red x on it

and the x is humans
or the x is a treasure map
which actually points to the chick
in a miniskirt tied to the wall who
Spiderman forgets to get back to

Whatever it is
that turns, boustrophedon,
into adults or astragals, glass
knuckle bones in the shape of goats'
vertebrae to win a dime on
Ox-turned ex-
words like a plow
six feet down

Four a.m.
They card the avenues
Help me up with the locks

What first held a cup
up to my name
bright   illegible
How many figures assumable

to pronounce: numbers are older than
        what numbers do, but it's not their fault
for inventing the body poorly, adding
neuron to nerve axon   What ease of women & men

half-won, half-worn, as wood, hard
when they discovered everything
was made of something
burnable   Elements
are mostly not amicable like M_2OH
says This tale is true &
innocent to a
fault   My plan is
to stay awake
with the weather which will
not

because a continent can take
no more human applicants Still

"I declare

  more beauty

  in your hair"

than smoke

d fish Don't worry

we're all here We won't laugh

while you sleep like I like a book that fits through my sleeve

but what would have to do with the ocean?

What would have to do with the sea?

ESSAY: *Delicately*

The father pollutes his body and
this is illegal and yet he does not
knowingly or purposefully pollute rivers
except by the small necessities
of daily living. Chevron pollutes rivers
and dirt and children are born
into brain cells in wrong places. If my father
smokes in a public place, this could
get him into trouble. If he shoots
heroin at home and someone
official finds him he
will be fined or arrested, maybe jailed.
This is the classic story in which a hero
sets out on a voyage, like Homer's or Dante's, and
along the way finds out something about
her / himself, only this time there's nothing
left to find out. For the world like Sappho was either

small, dark, and ugly
or small, dark, and beautiful.

ESSAY: *Ducks*

break what is the
     nectarine   —   word

No ideas but in
       what
       duck
in various parts of the world

     duck:
     tail of the duck   reflection of the duck

         = the duck of the gondola
       skating across surfaces of ducks

a troupe of carp below the surface of the pond follow
the duck like a herd
of oranges below because
a carp knows
where a duck
goes go crumbs below
the surface of the duck, the duck's
feet below
the water; on the surface of the water, trees
and underneath the trees, an orange herd of
oranges moves through trees, is it
trees in the water or trees in air? I distinguished the essence, not
the quality of objects, said Jean Genet, he
was always saying something, like Chief of the Underwear wondered
and wondered, making a poem
of the thought: dusks reflect you

ESSAY: *Beautiful*

live soldiers swimming through silver
water, pickled herring, the Sons
and Daughters
of Stanley, a can of
sardines; You, bony
beauty &
bed, bedclothes, the red
& yellow floor, a
beautiful green. Under the sheets his beautiful
knee rises and so rise
the knees of my people. Hey.
The beautiful mindless & quiet
stone at the bottom of this gray
river now quiet
in a dry room. Light
comes through and is
beautiful, too; so
the eyes of my people. My people
are bounding across highways toward
buses to drive through beautiful American
backroads, humming, they are blind. Bad-
ass beauty all
comfortable in the front
seat of my
pants'
car. Beauty thinks
she's so god-
like, beautiful, and
it is, loveliest of what pears I leave

behind on the kitchen counter with some keys that open things I need to get
into, like that dark, a miniature curved dinosaur sneeze, or a kernel
of corn melted just right. Home sound of hum about the appliances. A
comma. Brenda's carnival taffy. Yum.

STUDY: *How Night Might Be Strung*

were sight visible, ephemerable,

as the creatures close to the ground go

Night again

talking the knots out of rain

in a practice of Day again:

Day, & heys brightly, a riot

of color and time;

The firemen are stealing the fire—

Night again;   night;   Space,

collapsed between us.

ESSAY: *Ode*

A Pythagorean belief in numbers satisfied the need for symbols thinking of

music not as numbers but as sound a

weigh station from cosmology's

missals & breviaries, Let me invent you a language   two hundred notes per

vowel: Te Deum Ta

Dum Laudamus De

Laudid

singing I

dominate the conifers

& confitures and in the words of my father "Ha Ha" and in the words that be

-came the

hymn &

in his

cathedral

in Milan, St. Paul, I

knew you to be

imitated

& in the Ambrosian

& not just

biblically

& I knew you

to be of iambic

diameter

& thick as Ambro-

sani & liturgy &

I knew you as the vehicle's answer to history & art & of fertile creation,

cigars & long

& short noises

& syllables

sung
moved not with the singing

but with the thing sung

& the think sunk   sung think   and the think   the thung sink & who
deserves
to be known is

you along with
that of poetry philosophy
poetry poetry & architecture & poetry

ESSAY: *When I Think of Sex, a Moist Fog*

When I think of sex, some people
think of seals barking
but I think of shrimp and bleach.

When I think of sex with some people
I think of cones and rods, but they
think of flywheels.

When some people think of sex, they
think of plastic and rubber and frisbees
but when I think of them and sex I think

of International Ultimate Championships and
of grass stains on the knees
and flies and zippers, and xs

over their
eyes and they are dead and when I think

of them and sex I think I do not
want to have sex with a dead
person until I am dead.

ARTIFACT: *First of All, Sea; and Half of the Sea is Truth, Half Wind, Wonder*

1. It is wise to hearken not to me, but to my word, and to confess that all things are blank, or they are William Blake.

2. Eyes and ears are bad witnesses if men do not have women to understand they do not have souls. They do not have souls.

10. Nature loves a slide; a riding, gliding shiny atomic slide.

16. The learning of many things teacheth not understanding, else would it have taught Pythagoras and Popeye and again Sockeye salmon to survive.

19. . . . . . . to know the thought by which all thoughts are stirruped through all thoughts

20. This world, ... which . . . . . . is / was . . . . . . now, and ever shall be an ever-living, ever-loving what . . . . . . with measures of it kindling, and measures going out

23. Run to the gate . . . . . .
    . . . . . .
    you
    . . . . . . small, and of winter
    Stunned . . . . . . as of

    . . . . the surge of blue

ESSAY: *In the Land of What Dress*

I'd like to share this news:
where were you when we were getting hired?

                  (I was getting into
my scintillating towering super shiny super green metallic
   super duper iridescent bug dress I was wearing
     out of the forest to outshine
       you all (quietly)

I am stuck in the Land of What

Dress to Wear—:   Nice barn, nice house
Flags and poles, and flags and poles, but
                     Dear Midwest,

in the flat flat flatlands (in the) (heart-)

My poems made the low plains, the Cowpalace, move.

ESSAY: *I Said to My Leg (Be Still)*

I said to my head: Be kingly!
I said to my arm: Be majestic!
I said to my leg: Be so!

But there were certain muscles between the ankle and the knee
that could not submit & knew
nothing of the role they were asked to play. They continued
to express the insignificance of daily life, to show
themselves as muscle & tendon, not
flesh-made-light. The leg
began to ask itself:
Am I beautiful? Is this?
Is this admiration? Is this the richness
of color? The 14 bands of the globe?

ESSAY: *Color*

There is a magenta inside the snail, a red
medusa and a purple sun. There is a red thorn
in the esophagus where we chew our green

orange falling out of the sky and a light
body opening a transparent door or wing. This is Untitled
Pale Green. There is a certain body

in an uncertain envelope There is a trace of flesh is

it yes

a sky and a sun the size of a thumb.

There is a red body and its red fist flying (through black space) There is
an Untitled dream under the hill and black sky, a gold-
hill (red)

dream

with a hole in it. There is America Gray Blue. There is a shadow
behind white and a little yellow tobacco stain somewhere under the heart.

A man falls out of his shadow his arms are raised his face
I mean I saw his shadow mouth
open & blue toward the sides of the sky
with White and Other White

White has a turtle's name
a carapace with white diamonds on its back it has 3 hearts on the edge

4 if you count the one that's born or dying

There is a tiny green beneath the sun. It's us.

Upper Air has a no-frame frame of color around & footprints in and through
    a heart & a heart–
lump to the left

A man walks sideways (onto the screen) with two night-arms his thumbs are
    anatomically
incorrect, the ear–

hole open
(toward space).

This one's too big to look at, too blue, until an anterior return to calm
can change us we will have to keep them
in the Deep Orange Big Orange Big Blue and Black Museum.

The hearts are smashed (Deep Black) together with a bunch of birds (blue)
    (wings or not)
inside the black border
of black. There is Yellow here living inside
and out which I saw last night with my eyes

closed and all the colors

behind Deep Black.

There is a white hole in the sky and it's not snow It's showing chaos
onto the canvas now in a beautiful (bright) way like the result of a blind mechanic
Maybe he had to climb a ladder to paint that. The existence of empty permits this
movement, playing on the two

elemental gifts: matter (of atomic invisibility) and not. We had movement
to create the atomic combinations (science has proved this) into earth water
air fire and everything else had a tongue shooting out of blue

Don't let gods intervene in the march (of humans or the world)
for the inexplicable torments
they cause us. They have given us the Pleasure of Movement but have not
removed Pain from the world.

Where is the heart-branch in vertebrates? Does a snake have a heart and if so
    which kind?
A loud deep but not-deep sound (laughing) or (a heart)—

(For example how to detach the cerebral trunk from the respiratory drawer with,
    say, a bullet
to the mouth.

Now an open H., he forgot
to paint it closed he forgot
to put all the color to the heart and now we see right through it to the paper air We do
see a life jacket in the yellow surf We take it up, we move to it

In the Explication of That Which Is

Where there is a blue body falling
out of the sky headfirst toward the tiny
door (red-orange) with more blue-behind but it's not
a door—an arch, a great colossus through which

the body
won't move.

This was accidented on its way back
(from the space-document) and had to be split

(triptych).

Now it's raining colored space on the human

capsules making the colors (heart) bleed

The sun is bleeding a few wings into gray-green

which is a small patch & difficult like winter it won't be long now

till green or white or blue

in Lovely Blueness and most days I don't mind, I don't mind being

with all these humans.

This Yellow bell smeared into middle-blue (tiled sky) makes me dream of a tiger &

opens an eight-sided crystal room with 16 views

of time

There is a Blue Tower of Air exploding

A fire in the middle of the flower which is not yet beyond a pistil

A red eave of night, red night cave

A sideways, weeping eye

the (blue) vertebrae loosely gathered toward blue and rising (through) the (white) sky

We will argue about it
Mine about this or that
We will arrive toward yellow or blue
which color will serve as a receptacle
for feeling sifted (through) a salt-colored water The silt
of a feeling and (hold) it (meaning)

It's an old facet of me, an odd faucet I've never
seen I don't know I've always seen something
with my eyes closed

I wanted to frame myself inside a circle, a self-portrait tree

It all unites or unties in the 4th element & I see it
The light that makes the essential meaning
of dark or space, dark-space

Everything is in reverse and you learn it
backward Process transforming Plotted
forward

The dream is an ordering
of my life I said Well I better do something
with my hands, so I put my fist in my mouth

Now there's
Blue Spine on the edge
of Kimono held together between the companion of two
red wings. This butterfly is
a pile of them compressed under a great
mass of space is
we think trying to cut loose
but maybe they're moving
toward more tight
like a city Tied
to ground It could begin
to fly off now a black
boot of light holds us
down Who will
tear this (air) for us

There are (orange) knuckles at the top of the sky There are knuckles
trying to rip the sky off Blue
knuckles and a duck are trying
to hold it down I always thought of
you in terms of numbers and molecules

Color could swallow me, and tried to, a room from which to see
light all at once or time "This is my
studio" Working from the light of the paper tree
toward dark or

back again in an autonomy of melted cover parts
I had myself hidden in the lid from all bitterness From all bitterness
& saltiness comes / all / color

Another sun spills or spits its guts
It was the mother of me
I was ready to be done in
I got all dissolved

There is actually no perspective one can
point to, like trying to see
from the point-of-view of a leaf I just want to speak like a normal human so I will
for a minute You're so purty. That's no
cold idea but a nervous influx from between my 100 million
neurons and their ten
thousand synapses
I say this between the profound rut
in my brains: Alarming dogs did I
think up Love did I dream it
in my brain was it (Love)
born there, did Love originate between my head? You
remind me of my first Love whose eyes were green and he was
trouble, too. We used to maneuver through the descending motor orders
into marrow & sex before all this rifling
through the threads of thought There was

The Round World

ESSAY: *The Earliest World*

When the tired drones of TV sit-
coms finally graduate perhaps to
death will it be I hope soon but no, it's when the sun becomes
our red giant
sounding forth
froth universal.   I want to propose
the earliest world.   The earliest world was a
black place   Is this because
her eyes were closed?
The earliest world was always inside Is this
because it was dark in there?
The earliest world was vaulting
black in there the sky A spirit thrown back
upon itself   Media's no cricket.
In the earliest world I said I did not think
now I go into the sun now
I will switch off the light
In the earliest world there were clouds
moving across a blank black sky
Are you short?

World, are you?

Are you, shorty?

Are you sweet?
As the business of the future is being dangerous, please
In the earliest world, would I could look up at the sky and there was the
sky—vipers and winged snakes . . .   I could never not think of it

as the sky but
I could look

In the earliest world there was someone
jogging along the foot
path but she
was not wearing Gore-tex. If the vipers
increased as fast as their nature would allow, impossible it were for man
to maintain himself here
on earth, much less
humans   There were so
many early worlds I am losing
them now. Oops,
there goes a world, a
cash register with ladybugs, gone. Departed, black
urchins with their
tingling thorns, a shady world
under the eucalyptus trees with apple-flavored yogurt
for your birthday party; departed, the generous Troad, realm of my
barn owl backbones. There
is another one, a dark
room with puppy
shit where I perform
headstands against
the wall, naked. Who are the humans? Where are
the snakes? These are all worlds, gone.

REPRISAL: *Building (Beautifuls)*

In the building of beautifuls, sunflowers
are building bikes and mini-
bikes, and build dogs that bark and echo off hills
Little plots of straw are building a gray horse, and
dapples, sunlight. The olive
tree builds ripe pears and fingernails, while corn over flat land is building castles
with cattles inside and beans over curved
build houses and tanks and trucks, on little
jeweled plots each one fitting right up
to the next. Black figs build a drainage ditch, and swimming pools, fields
of rape build Germans (whoops),
and green the water, peas make
a palm tree sign saying Nuclear Free Zone
and museum sites, barley makes meaningful
statements in manly
ornament and empires eating
peoples; factories make poisoned
bodies, cherries, humans
beat the trickery
out of the sea. Someone builds red bugs wing by wing. I've seen that
traveler before, the whore
from the Carian sewer takes pleasure in her human
rhetoric, Cicero, a carcass
was round and sweet and lived
in tangles of trees, building
housings right up to the water, the sea
over Brittany, Normandy; Doricha, your bones
fell asleep long ago for they say they saw and loved
many, and were captivated by all things beautiful, humans

ESSAY: *Parts of Plants, Animals, Physics*

every time I want(ed) to read in a sort of
cardboard box sun cum how many minutes between
one & 12:15
I see myself thus speaking
or spake under whose
shadow like the
reflection from a glycerin cradle

(there was) fires yanked out by a grand colorist
or color yanked out or orange
yanked from the instability of orange
or
the atmosphere
or
the

the
sun
domain of

despite the men on Avenue D & heliogravures etched
into each address (the world's involuntary radiography)

What can the Eternal declare?
(All the flowers of chemical reaction were there)

Now I'm getting something to blow you up